ten Zen seconds

Twelve incantations for purpose,
power and calm

Eric Maisel

SOURCEBOOKS, INC.®
NAPERVILLE, ILLINOIS

Published by Sourcebooks, Inc.
P.O. Box 4410, Naperville, Illinois 60567–4410
(630) 961–3900
FAX: (630) 961–2168
www.sourcebooks.com

Library of Congress in Publication
Maisel, Eric
  Ten Zen seconds : twelve incantations for purpose, power and calm / Eric Maisel.
    p. cm.
  ISBN-13: 978-1-4022-0853-9
  ISBN-10: 1-4022-0853-7
  1. Stress management. 2. Breathing exercises. I. Title.

RA785.M34 2007
613'.192—dc22

                                                    2006100789

           Printed and bound in the United States of America
                 VP 10 9 8 7 6 5 4 3 2 1

for Ann, as always

Table of Contents

Chapter One

Introducing Ten Zen Seconds

I am going to teach you a centering technique that verges on the miraculous. You can dramatically improve your ability to center, become more calm and more powerful, and radically improve your life by taking ten-second pauses of the sort that I'm about to describe. You'll be amazed to learn that such a life-altering strategy can come in a span as small as ten seconds, but it can! Hundreds of my clients, and hundreds of volunteers, have used this technique to center, calm, and ground themselves while waiting in traffic, sitting in the dentist's office, preparing to record a new album, or readying themselves to talk to their teenager. They know firsthand that this technique works.

This ten-second technique has two components: a breathing part and a thinking part. The basis of Ten Zen Seconds is using a single deep breath as a container for a specific thought. First you practice deep breathing until you can produce a breath that lasts about five seconds on the inhale and five seconds on the exhale. Learning to do this will take you only a few minutes. Then you insert a thought into the breath, silently thinking half the thought on the inhale and half the thought on the exhale. This, too, will take you only a short time to learn. In an afternoon you can familiarize yourself with the program outlined in this book.

If this ten-second centering technique sounds very simple, it's because it is: It is simple to grasp, simple to practice, simple to use, and simple to master. It's nevertheless profound in its benefits. You will be able to do things that previously felt too painful or too difficult to attempt. You will be able to calm and center yourself before an important meeting or conversation. You will change your basic attitudes about life—moving from pessimism to optimism, procrastination to effort, and worry to calm. These are the benefits that await you.

I'm adapting a word from the world of magic—incantation—to describe these breath-and-thought bundles. An incantation is a ritual recitation of a verbal charm meant to produce a magical effect. Those are exactly our methods and our aims. The magical effects are instant centering and instant calm. The ritual we use is breathing a certain way and thinking a certain thought for ten seconds at a time. The verbal charms are the specific thoughts that I'll teach you, with twelve incantations in all.

I hope that you're a little skeptical about the promises I'm making. By all means hold on to your skepticism! Then, when you see that ten-second centering works, it'll strike you as all the more magical.

Marrying East and West

We know from Eastern practices like yoga and meditation the importance of the twin concepts of breath awareness and mindfulness. Breath awareness is simply paying attention to the way we breathe while reminding ourselves to breathe more deeply and more fully than we usually do. As we rush through life we breathe shallowly, as our mind chatter propels us forward. Burdened by what Buddhists call "monkey mind"—that worried, needy, grasping, anxious, unaware mind of the everyday person—we fall into the habit of automatic shallow breathing.

A vicious cycle evolves where we maintain this shallow breathing as a defense against knowing our own thoughts. In a corner of consciousness we know that if we were to slow down and breathe deeply we would become fully aware of our thoughts and learn too much about what we're actually thinking. Out of a fear that acquiring such an understanding would upset us, we make sure not to engage in deep breathing.

If we were willing to engage in conscious deep breathing, we would become more mindful. We would begin to see our own tricks; how what we hold as facts are mere opinions, how our usual ways of operating often sabotage us, and how pain, resentment, and disappointment course through our system. Therefore, mindfulness is much easier to champion as an abstract idea than it is to tolerate in reality. Mindfulness implies that we grow aware of how our mind actually operates, which is a scary proposition.

I'm employing a very simple version of breath awareness as a core element of Ten Zen Seconds. You have nothing arcane to learn, no long sitting meditations to endure, no distinctions to make between emptying your mind and concentrating. You will simply learn and practice one long, deep breath, a breath longer and fuller than you usually experience. This addition to your breathing repertoire is all you need to take from Eastern practice in order to begin your transformation to mindfulness and centeredness.

From Western thought I'm taking the basic ideas of cognitive therapy. The main idea of cognitive therapy is that what we say to ourselves—our self-talk—is the primary way we maintain our problems, defenses, flaws, and blocks. If we manage to change our self-talk we have done something profound, something more substantial than just making some innocent linguistic alterations.

The twelve incantations I'll teach you function the way that "thought substitutes" function in cognitive therapy. A cognitive therapist (and I am one) teaches you to identify maladaptive self-talk, confront and dispute wrong thinking, and substitute new language that supports your intention to move in a certain direction. You learn to notice your characteristic forms of distorted thinking and create thought substitutes that in form and content are indistinguishable from affirmations. These are key ideas from cognitive therapy that underpin Ten Zen Seconds.

Ten-second centering does not demand a full practice of mindful meditation or a complete course in cognitive therapy. In an important sense I have done that work for you by presenting you with twelve incantations that you might have arrived at yourself through insight meditation, self-reflection, pain, and suffering. When, for instance, I teach you the incantation "I expect nothing" and explain to you why it is important to let go of expectations, though not of goals or dreams, I will be presenting an idea that you might have arrived at through years of ardent practice. The practice has been done for you and you can reap the benefits.

This is not an illegitimate shortcut. Suffering is overrated. I would prefer that you change your life in a day and not in a decade. I hope that you agree. I hope that you concur that you have already earned your merit badges in suffering and that it is legitimate to quickly learn a way of centering that works, rather than arriving at one by studying everything that the East and the West have to offer.

Being Uncentered

Centered and *uncentered* are useful words that conjure a way of dividing our experiences into the kinds that we want to nurture and the kinds that we hope to avoid. We would prefer to feel less scattered, chaotic, distracted, anxious, nervous, irritable, and unsettled. We would like to be able to marshal our inner resources, focus our attention, make strong decisions, and act when action is required. We would love to feel more grounded, centered, and calm. People understand these distinctions without needing to have them explained. However, until you take the time to describe your own experience of uncenteredness in writing, you won't possess a clear personal picture. Do that right now. Take a few minutes and describe what it feels like when you're uncentered.

Here are some reports from clients and study subjects. Jessica, a painter, explained, "When I feel uncentered I feel chaotic, fragmented, and unable to move forward. There is an ominous feeling of impending failure and a keen sense of paralysis." Linda, a social worker, described this unwelcome state in the following way: "When I'm uncentered I feel off-balance, as if I can't right myself. I feel like I'm searching for something but I'm completely lost. Sometimes my uncenteredness manifests itself as disorientation, confusion, or, worst of all, disconnection from my emotions."

Annie, a poet from the Ozarks, described her experience metaphorically: I'm floating along a calm river, watching birds, marveling at the stark beauty of the limestone bluffs, when at a bend in the river I get caught in a roiling eddy. In the force of the whirling vortex my self-esteem is torn away. I'm spinning so fast I can't focus. I tell myself, 'If you paddle, you can get out of this,' and I reply, 'I can't paddle well enough, so there's no point.'"

Why is it so important that we rid ourselves of uncenteredness? First, we have accidents that we might otherwise avoid, both mental and physical. Second, when we're uncentered we do things that we regret, things that come from the shadowy parts of our personality. We make some of our biggest decisions—to marry, to pursue a new career, to move to a different city—while uncentered. Stop now and write about the mistakes that you've made and the accidents that have befallen you while you were uncentered. Stopping to remember these painful experiences will help remind you why you are spending time with this book and committing to learning how to center.

Traditional Solutions

Most people don't know what to do to center themselves and simply hope and pray that their anxiety, agitation, and confusion will pass of its own accord. Some try to alter their state of uncenteredness chemically, risking addiction and achieving something very different from the experience of centeredness. A large majority of people do not even recognize that they're uncentered; they either accept their rushed, harried, fractured state as the norm or misname their uncenteredness as personal style. They think of themselves as "just anxious," "overly sensitive," "obsessive-compulsive," "a worrier," and so on, not realizing that their uncenteredness is a state and not a trait.

Possessing no solutions, possessing only ineffective solutions, and not being aware of the problem are the usual ways we deal with uncenteredness. A minority of people are aware that they need to center and try to practice healthy methods of grounding themselves. They try meditation, yoga, tai chi, and other practices that share a commitment to slowing down, reducing mental chatter, and becoming present. People who try these methods almost always find them valuable. They also typically report that these helpful strategies are hard to sustain over time and hard to employ in real-life situations.

Barbara, a singer from Chicago, complained, "I practice tai chi, yoga, and qigong regularly, plus my own form of meditation. I have routines that are part of my day that are designed to keep me centered, and I currently spend some time each evening meditating and reflecting on the day's events. This keeps my general stress level low. And still I don't have a mental practice that I can call on when I'm really off-center and need to shift my state of mind on the spot."

Traditional solutions tend to require time—a half hour listening to a relaxation tape, fifteen minutes going through postures, twenty minutes quieting mind chatter—and are not designed to be used in public. They do not help you center, except in a residual or cumulative way, when your boss throws a new project on your desk, your daughter tells you that she's just been in a fender-bender, or you feel scattered and anxious during an important meeting.

Leslie, a small business owner in Ontario, observed, "I've created several guided meditations that I currently use to calm myself, to regain my confidence, and to bring me back to the present moment.

I simply put on some relaxing music and visualize my way through one of these meditations. This works wonderfully but it takes at least a half hour, which I don't always have. I would love to find something that can bring me to a similar place but doesn't take so long."

Traditional solutions fall short for an even more important reason—they have no thought component. They help you relax, focus your mind, calm your nerves, and so on, but they are not designed to meet your centering challenges by providing you with a repertoire of useful thoughts. We need certain thoughts if we are to center ourselves, specifically the dozen thoughts I'll name shortly. For instance, we need to make use of the power of the phrase "I am completely stopping" when we find ourselves rushing around. We need to hear ourselves say, "I expect nothing," before an important presentation, so as to make our points clearly, compassionately, and powerfully. Phrases of this sort are crucial components of a real centering program.

Many people grow frustrated in their attempts to use traditional solutions like yoga or meditation and conclude that they are doomed to never feel centered. Lucinda, a painter from Milwaukee, explained, "I've tried many things, but nothing seems to keep me focused. Sometimes I feel that being centered is something that just happens to a fortunate few, while the rest of us are doomed to wander around in a daze." Ten Zen Seconds ends that frustration. It is quick, effective, easy to learn, and easy to acquire. Let's get going and look at its two main components: breathing and thinking.

Chapter Two

Breathing and Thinking

The "ten-second" part of ten-second centering refers to a single breath of ten seconds' duration that you use as a container to hold a specific thought. The first thing I'd like you to do is familiarize yourself with what ten seconds feels like. Take some time right now and observe the second hand of your watch or your wall clock. Experience ten seconds. Really feel each second. Be patient and observant and repeat the process a few times until you get a good, visceral sense of ten seconds.

What I think you'll notice is that ten seconds is a significant amount of time and even a surprisingly long amount of time. It probably feels longer and more substantial than you expected it would. Each second of the ten seconds is a distinct entity, clearly separate and distinguishable from the one that preceded it and the one that followed it. Five seconds, the increment of time between the one and the two on the dial face, is its own distinct entity, made distinct because of the way a dial face is designed. Ten seconds, the increment of time between the one and the three, is likewise a clear, contained unit.

The customary breath you take is on the order of two or three seconds in duration. This is normal, natural, automatic, and does a fine job of keeping you alive. Exactly because it is natural and automatic, a breath of this length does nothing to interrupt your mind chatter, alter your sense of a given situation, or support change. When you consciously decide to breathe more slowly and deeply, you alert your body to the fact that you want it to behave differently. You are not just changing your breathing pattern, you are making a full-body announcement that you are entering into a different relationship with your mind and your body.

The long, deep, ten-second breath that you take as part of the ten-second centering process serves as a container for specific thoughts. Before it does that, it serves as the very best way available to you to stop what you are doing and thinking. If you have been doing something compulsive and harmful to yourself, this alteration in breathing gives you the chance to bring awareness to your behavior. If you have been obsessively worrying about something, the conscious production of one long, deep breath interrupts your mind flow and provides you with a golden opportunity to counter your anxious thoughts.

A long, deep breath is the equivalent of a full stop and the key to centering. There are certain considerations with respect to producing this long, deep breath. The first is whether to breathe through your nose or through your mouth. I suggest that you inhale through your nose and also exhale through your nose, keeping your lips lightly shut. As with the other suggestions I'll be offering, I think your best policy is to try it my way a few times before making any changes. Once you've given my method a reasonable try, by all means personalize and customize your breath so that it suits your style and physiology.

The next matter is whether to keep your eyes open or shut. I suggest that you close them so as to shut out the visual stimuli around you. This will increase the benefits you obtain from deep breathing and, when you introduce a thought into the deep breath, will allow you to focus on the thought without distraction. You can either sit or stand, but I recommend that in the beginning you practice your deep breathing while seated in a chair, with your feet planted squarely on the ground.

Your inhale should last about five seconds and your exhale another five seconds. If you have experience with traditional practices, you will know that many of them ask you to concentrate on the inhale and let the exhale take care of itself. I suggest that you give the inhale and the exhale equal weight and equal consideration. Each is going to serve as a container for "half a thought" and each needs attention. You'll want to inhale slowly and deeply, pause slightly before you exhale (this pause, too, is important), and exhale in the same slow, deep, controlled way that you inhaled. Practice until you have this long, deep breath—inhale and exhale both—under your conscious control.

> Practice now. Practice taking a long, deep breath, five seconds on the inhale and five seconds on the exhale. Do this several times.

You may want to build up to your long, deep breath. Use a few preliminary breaths to progressively deepen your breathing pattern. I predict that ultimately you'll find this unnecessary and that you'll be able to switch from your ordinary breathing-and-thinking pattern to your centering incantation from one breath to the next. For now, though, if progressively breathing more deeply helps you to arrive at a long, deep breath, by all means allow yourself some warm-up breaths.

The first few times you practice producing a long, deep breath you may notice that you're rushing yourself or that anxiety or stray thoughts are preventing you from patiently inhaling and patiently exhaling. Try to consciously quiet your body and your mind. Suggest to yourself that you grow calmer, more peaceful, and more focused. If you have ongoing trouble producing a long, deep breath, you might try counting slowly to five on the inhale and five on the exhale. Two slow, unrushed counts of five should produce the deep inhale and the deep exhale that make up one long, deep breath.

> Please practice again right now. Don't read on until you've "mastered" one long, deep breath. It's the basis of Ten Zen Seconds and the only physical component of the program. If you find it hard or awkward in the beginning, just keep practicing. You'll master it if you give it an honorable try.

Welcome back from your practice. I hope that it went well. If you do nothing more than incorporate a few long, deep breaths into your day you will become more centered. For example Sandi, a study subject, explained, "When I first learned to actually breathe (at age thirty-seven!), I remember that it made such a huge change in my life. I'd had no clue how much I was holding back and how pinched and sour my breathing actually was. Now, six years later, I'm a much more relaxed person."

Lenore, a musician, explained, "This exercise was easy for me, as several years ago I learned breathing techniques to master control over anxiety and panic issues. I am currently a practitioner of yoga as well as a teacher, and I know that breath is the key to everything. Breath is the first thing I teach my students. I had to take several long cleansing/releasing breaths before I could actually focus on 'one long, deep breath,' but then I felt energy and warmth coming into my body."

Francine, an environmental lawyer, reported, "At the beginning I felt a bit of dizziness so I started counting as suggested, which took my focus away from being dizzy. I was managing well by the sixth go but wanting to know what came next. I got rather impatient with this practice exercise and my mind was saying, 'Okay, I've got this, what's the next bit? Do I have to do the same thing over and over again?' I realized that this is how I approach a lot of things in my life!"

Your tendency to rush on may prevent you from engaging with and mastering this first step. Don't let that tendency derail you here at the beginning. Your only job right now is to practice taking long, deep breaths and working through any obstacles that arise to deep breathing. Those obstacles may include physical ones like dizziness or mental ones like the thought that this is boring or silly. Overcome those obstacles by continuing to practice. Say to yourself, "I am willing to give this a real shot." If some obstacle to deep breathing remains, have a conversation with yourself about why that obstacle may have arisen and what you can do to eliminate it.

Breathing and Thinking

The meat of ten-second centering is using the long, deep breath you just mastered as a container to hold a specific thought. Let's consider two different sorts of thoughts: "stained-glass window" and "I am perfectly fine." One task you face when you insert a thought into a long, deep breath is deciding how to break it up so that it divides naturally and rhythmically between the inhale and the exhale. You'll discover, for instance, that "stained-glass window" divides most naturally as (stained-glass) and (window) and that "I am perfectly fine" divides most naturally as (I am perfectly) and (fine). Give this a try and see if you agree.

The most natural way to break up a given phrase is not by mechanically dividing it in half according to its number of syllables but by testing it out and allowing it to divide as it wants. Consider the seven-syllable phrase "a brisk walk in the country," which, because it contains seven syllables, can't be divided equally. As an exercise, try to divide this phrase up so that it comfortably fills one long breath. I think you'll discover that it naturally divides into (a brisk walk) on the inhale and (in the country) on the exhale. Any other division of these seven syllables feels awkward and unnatural. Try some variations, like (a brisk) on the inhale and (walk in the country) on the exhale and (a brisk walk in) on the inhale and (the country) on the exhale. I bet these won't feel right to you.

A second challenge is inserting a thought into your long, deep breath but not seeing an accompanying image. When we think a thought, sometimes we see an accompanying image and sometimes we don't. "Stained-glass window" is the kind of phrase that naturally conjures an image. "I am perfectly fine" is the kind of phrase that doesn't tend to spark an image. The centering incantations you will learn are of the second type and you should have no problem "not seeing" images as you breathe-and-think. If you're a very visual person and accompany all of your thoughts with images, you'll want to make an effort to "think without seeing." Part of the meditative and centering power of this technique is in the way that it reduces mental stimuli and clutter, including unnecessary visual information.

Let's practice breathing-and-thinking right now. First, practice your long, deep breath. Then insert each of the following phrases into a single long breath, letting the word or phrase divide naturally between the inhale and the exhale:

"Stained-glass window"

"I am perfectly fine"

"A brisk walk in the country"

"I am an artist"

"Amazing"

"A special meal with my best friend and her two cousins"

"Big dog"

"I am calm and contented"

"Two toads and an alligator"

I'm sure that you noticed several things. Single words (like "amazing") and short phrases (like "big dog") had to be stretched to fill up a long breath. With "big dog," for instance, you were actually thinking "biiiiiiiig" on the inhale and "dooooooooog" on the exhale. A long phrase like "a special meal with my best friend and her two cousins" could hardly be squeezed in at all. Some phrases may have surprised you by their power, others by their ability to make you smile.

Amanda, a reporter, explained, "I found that if the phrase was rhythmic and evenly divided, it was easy to do. If it wasn't, I had problems. Either I sped the breath up too much or my mind went off on a tangent. For instance, I bounced from one image of a stained-glass window to another and ended up at the cathedral of Notre Dame. Before I knew it I was off thinking about French food and wine. This was a lovely mini-vacation but not exactly centering!"

Set aside a little time to practice breathing-and-thinking. Create some phrases of your own and pop each one into a long, deep breath. Learn the nuances of splitting up phrases so that they naturally and comfortably fit into the container that a long, deep breath creates. Practice this process, enjoy it, and don't read on until you've given it at least a few minutes of your time.

Chapter Three

The Twelve Incantations

We're ready now to look at the twelve incantations. Each one is an independent centering charm that you can use according to the situation you find yourself in, the problem you face, or your particular experience of uncenteredness. I'll introduce the incantations in this chapter and explain them in detail in subsequent chapters. I suspect that you'll intuitively understand the meaning and purpose of each one as soon as you encounter it. Whether or not you do, you'll have the opportunity to learn more about them as we proceed.

I'll use parentheses to indicate how I believe each incantation naturally divides. Please note that Incantation 3 functions differently from the other eleven. It's a "name your work" incantation. You think something different each time you employ it, depending on the work you intend to accomplish. For instance, if your work is an imminent performance, your phrase might be (I am ready) (to sing) or (this audition) (will be excellent). I'm using (I am) (doing my work) as a place-marker to stand for the idea that you name specific work each time you use this incantation.

Here are the twelve incantations:
1. (I am completely) (stopping)
2. (I expect) (nothing)
3. (I am) (doing my work)
4. (I trust) (my resources)
5. (I feel) (supported)
6. (I embrace) (this moment)
7. (I am free) (of the past)
8. (I make) (my meaning)
9. (I am open) (to joy)
10. (I am equal) (to this challenge)
11. (I am) (taking action)
12. (I return) (with strength)

Try these incantations out right now. Go through the list slowly, incorporating each phrase into its own long, deep breath. Begin with some preparatory centering breaths, breathe-and-think the first thought (I am completely) (stopping), and pause for reflection before moving on to the next incantation. Take your time and begin to experience the power of these twelve phrases.

Let me give you a brief overview of the twelve incantations by describing how one client used them. Jane, a singer, songwriter, and actress who specialized in musical theater, presented a variety of issues when she came to see me in my capacity as a creativity coach. She had severe performance anxiety issues, had been raised in a critical and rejecting household, felt anxious about the quality of her voice and her inability to assert herself, and wanted help centering herself before auditions. We worked together in a variety of ways, including my teaching her ten-second centering and Jane employing the twelve incantations in real-life situations. Here's how she put them to use:

1. (I am completely) (stopping)

Jane was aware that she kept herself in a rush, always piling activity upon activity, and that by keeping herself in a rush she rarely got around to practicing her audition pieces, either her songs or her monologues. She decided to use (I am completely) (stopping) once a day, about an hour after she got home from work, to check in with herself to see if she was ready to rehearse and practice. Most evenings she wasn't. But about twice a week she found that by completely stopping, an opening occurred that allowed her to face her fears and rehearse. After about six weeks she felt her confidence build to the point that she could return to auditioning. Jane also used Incantation 1 as a way to "completely stop" her racing, out-of-control thoughts right before auditions and performances.

2. (I expect) (nothing)

Jane realized that she was in the habit of putting extra pressure on herself by caring so much about landing the roles for which she auditioned. Caring so much caused her to get ungrounded and uncentered and raised her anxiety level tremendously, which invariably led to a weak audition. To interrupt this vicious cycle, she began using Incantation 2 to remind herself that her best bet was to audition "without expectations." She found that the instant she closed her eyes, practiced her deep breathing, and inserted Incantation 2 into a long, deep breath, she became calmer and more present. She also found it useful to use Incantation 2 before seeing her parents, as it inoculated her against the disappointment and pain she inevitably felt after interacting with them.

3. (I am) (doing my work)

Jane realized that forthrightly announcing that she had performing work to do and framing that work in a positive light helped strengthen and calm her. She created personalized incantations like (I am ready) (to sing), (This audition) (will be excellent), and (I am excited) (to be acting) and used them throughout the day, even while at her day job. These versions of Incantation 3 helped keep her in a positive mood and counteracted the negative thoughts that were always ready to infiltrate her system. If she heard about an actor's success and felt envious or if she lost out on an audition, she would breathe-and-think, (My work) (is to continue), a version of Incantation 3 that she used increasingly often.

4. (I trust) (my resources)

Jane knew that even when she was adequately prepared to perform, she nevertheless rarely felt adequately prepared. She began to use Incantation 4 to remind herself (and to convince herself) that once she was prepared, it was time to trust her skills and her training and proceed with confidence. She also used Incantation 4 to counteract the feeling that the odds against her were too long, that the industry was too whimsical and too cruel, and that she was not one of the lucky or connected ones. She recognized that such thoughts, even if true, only sapped her energy and killed her motivation and therefore needed blocking and replacing.

5. (I feel) (supported)

Like many people, Jane couldn't sort out her contradictory thoughts and feelings about spirituality, religion, and the meaning of life. She doubted that she believed in gods and consequently called herself agnostic. But she wasn't at all sure what she truly believed or felt, nor could she picture a way to get clear and arrive at convincing conclusions. She wasn't interested in joining a new church or reading books on spiritual healing and had decided to put all of that on a back burner. At the same time, the universe felt very cold to her. To counteract that coldness, she began employing Incantation 5, which began to serve as her sole spiritual practice.

6. (I embrace) (this moment)

Jane recognized that before performances and especially before auditions, she would catch herself wishing that she were somewhere—anywhere—else. She knew that this was a counterproductive thought and even an irrational one, as she was entirely instrumental in choosing her career and had done everything in her power to get herself to this place in the wings. She knew that she wanted to "change her mind" about not wanting to be there and began to use Incantation 6 for that purpose. By using Incantation 6 she could surrender, accept that she was exactly where she wanted to be, and relax.

7. (I am free) (of the past)

When Jane landed a role in a musical comedy and began rehearsing her part, which involved a lot of dancing as well as singing and acting, she found herself internally bombarded with messages from the past about her clumsiness. Her parents had laughed at her at her first dance recital, a memory that still haunted her. She knew that it was insane to suppose that dancing awkwardly at the age of seven meant that she couldn't dance, yet she'd never gotten over the sense that she was doomed as a dancer. All through the rehearsal process she turned to Incantation 7 when negative thoughts and feelings about her dancing threatened to derail her.

8. (I make) (my meaning)

Jane realized that she had gotten into the habit of second-guessing her motives for performing and by doing that would precipitate serious crises of meaning. This second-guessing occurred most often after visits with her parents, who never failed to remind her that she should have chosen a more sensible career. She would defend herself to them, arrive home, and feel severely depressed. In that dark mood, she would doubt herself and her choices. Previously she had no simple way to affirm that she really did believe in her meaning-making efforts and that she intended to stand behind her choices. Then she began using Incantation 8. By using this incantation when she felt her resolve slip or existential doubt creep into her thinking, she found it possible to recover her "meaning" center.

9. (I am open) (to joy)

As a child, Jane had experienced joy many times, even through such simple activities as looking up at the night sky or swimming in the neighborhood pool. As an adult, joy had become so elusive that she'd stopped expecting to experience it. That seemed to be the adult thing to do, to give up on joy and settle for "not too much unpleasantness" instead. Ultimately, though, that felt as unacceptable as settling for a life without love or hope. She knew that there was joy to be found in the present moment if only she could surrender to it, and joy to be found in performance. Once she realized that experiencing joy soothed and centered her and that it was her job to open up to its possibility, she committed to using Incantation 9 first thing every morning and regularly throughout the day.

10. (I am equal) (to this challenge)

Living a principled life, manifesting our potential, and realizing our goals and dreams constitute a recipe for challenge. Jane realized that she had to let go of the hope that things would be easy so as to avoid feeling uncentered when things turned out to not be easy. She knew that she was challenging herself by choosing to perform and by testing her mettle in an environment as competitive as show business. She therefore had to affirm that she was equal to that challenge, even if on a given day she didn't feel or believe that she was. Incantation 10 became a centering affirmation that she used on the spur of the moment, to remind herself that she had what it took to succeed.

11. (I am) (taking action)

Like many people, Jane knew that if she let herself drift into a passive, brooding way of being, as she regularly did, she would become depressed and uncentered. Although she knew that taking action—sometimes any action, just getting dressed and getting out the door—often completely lightened her mood and helped her re-center, it hadn't struck her just how important it was to take action to fight anxiety and doubt. When she made that connection, she immediately incorporated Incantation 11 into her daily routine, using it to counteract blue feelings and move past procrastination.

12. (I return) (with strength)

Jane found herself performing in a musical where she had to make many exits and entrances. Each new entrance provoked a bout of performance anxiety, which she began to quell by using Incantation 12. By announcing to herself that she was returning to the stage with strength, she blocked her anxious thoughts and inoculated herself against her main fear, that she would lose control of her body (a common fear among performers). She also began to use Incantation 12 as her main "transition" incantation throughout the day, especially when she returned from lunch and had to face a long afternoon of routine busywork.

I hope that Jane's experience gives you a sense of how ten-second centering works. Practice the twelve incantations a few times right now. Taking them one at a time, ask yourself the question, "When might I use this incantation?" Picture real-life situations and imagine yourself using one or another of the incantations before the situation, during it, and/or after it. If you feel ready, turn this mental practice into real practice by using one or two of the incantations in situations that arise for you today.

incantation 1:
i am completely stopping

We all rush around, prodded and pulled by our multiple duties and responsibilities. We're doing too many things and worrying too much. Many of us are also in a mad rush because we're running away from noticing the extent to which we're not living the life we'd hoped to lead. Rather than realizing our dreams, doing our deepest work, and making sufficient meaning, we keep ourselves in perpetual mental and physical motion.

The only way to stop running is to demand of ourselves that we stop running. We must tell ourselves to stop. Either we come to a complete stop or we keep rushing headlong toward our next task, our next worry, and our next depression. You come to a complete stop by using Incantation 1, "I am completely stopping." You think "I am completely" on the inhale, pause, and think "stopping" on the exhale. Then, and only then, will you actually stop.

You want the experience of coming to a complete stop, not just the experience of thinking some words. If the words "I am completely stopping" do not actually cause you to stop, the incantation is not doing its necessary work. If you do not believe in the idea of completely stopping, if you fear stopping so much that you don't mean it when you say it, or if you can't quite grasp the concept, then you will need to do some preliminary work on practicing stopping. You will need to buy into the idea. Do that preliminary work right now. Make a cup of tea, find a comfortable place to sit, and come to grips with the question, "Do I have permission to completely stop?" Wrestle with your resistance to stopping until you can honestly say that you agree that completely stopping is important and honestly feel emotionally equal to stopping.

Try Incantation 1 now. Repeat it a few times. Then make some notes to yourself about the thoughts and feelings that arose in you when you tried to completely stop. You may have met your darkest fears, largest worries, and gravest disappointments. You may have heard yourself say, "I need a drink," "I hate this," "I have too much to do," or, "This is ridiculous." Right now, replace thoughts of this sort with, "I'm not afraid of stopping," and, "It's about time that I stopped." Talk yourself into the belief that completely stopping is vital to your mental and physical well-being. After you've had this chat with yourself, repeat Incantation 1 a few times and see if you can really stop.

Using Incantation 1

Here are some reports from clients and study subjects who have put Incantation 1 into practice.

KATHERINE

"I can tell that my fear stands in the way of me completing stopping. I've been on the run all of my life. I've been on the run from myself and from the trauma I've carried with me since my childhood. My own existence reminds me of this trauma, so therefore I am on the run from myself. But it's no longer a good solution to run from boyfriends, jobs, apartments, tasks, from everything. This really must change and that's why I've committed to using Incantation 1."

Will some demon memory catch you if you completely stop? Can you let go of that fear or brave that fear?

KRISTIN

"What usually gets in the way of me completely stopping is a compulsion to 'get things done' or else my need to run away from something that's difficult to face. For a few moments after using Incantation 1, I experienced incredible relief. But it wasn't long before I was plagued again by thoughts of all the things I 'should, need, or want to be doing.' I have much more work to do on this!"

Are you in the grip of these same twin vises, the compulsion to get things done and the need to run away from difficult thoughts and feelings? Picture in your mind's eye the first vise opening. Turn the vise handle slowly and release the grip on your compulsion. Feel the compulsion to get things done release, dissipate, and vanish. Now picture the second vise opening and with it your need to run away. Do this work in your mind's eye, getting out of the vise grip of whatever stands between you and completely stopping.

SAM

"I take this incantation to mean that I am not just temporarily setting aside the endless to-do list of aspiration and work and daily life, but truly believing that the present moment is already good, that there is no need for it to be improved upon or altered. What stands in the way of me completely stopping is a sense that work and life are a treadmill moving faster and faster, that standing still means that I am falling behind. There is also a sense that I should be more than I already am, which is a feeling that dissolves when you examine it and see that it's based on nothing and means nothing."

Do you feel like you're on a treadmill that can't be stopped? Calmly picture yourself on that relentless treadmill. Feel yourself reaching toward the control pad and punching the automatic slow-down button. Feel the treadmill gradually slow down. Really feel the experience of stage-by-stage slowing. Feel it stop. Calmly step off the treadmill and towel yourself off.

GABRIELLA

"Why do I avoid stopping completely? What stands in the way most often is my mind, which is usually like a rubber suction cup on everything around me: my husband and his moods, my job, the cats, the dirty laundry, telephone and email messages to return, 'whose birthday is it this week?' and things like that. Mostly, I don't stop completely because I don't want to stop being 'me'—as though there is a certain amount of psychic focus required at all times to maintain my identity. Trying Incantation 1, a lot of childhood is surfacing and I feel the impulse to scream. I also wonder, are we sure that stopping completely isn't like dying? I think it is like dying. And we're all terrified of that. So it looks like it's not an easy thing to want to stop completely. But wait—it's the part of me that gives up easily that is saying that. These ramblings are coming from a part of me that I'm usually not supposed to talk about. This is both excellent and very scary."

Do you sense that you "suction" onto one thing after another in order to maintain your identity? You know how hard it is to remove a suction cup by pulling hard. But if you gently twist it, it comes away effortlessly. Picture yourself gently twisting rather than violently pulling. Gently release one "suctioned" worry after another until you're not worried about anything. You will notice that you have completely stopped—and that you still have an identity.

JODY

"Completely stopping had no meaning for me until two years ago when I moved away from San Diego and the life I had created there—a hectic, unhappy, unfulfilled, empty life. Finally I had the guts to leave a tenured position with benefits and retirement. I knew that if I stayed I would not live to use the retirement. Here I am today, living in a cabin built in 1937. My day begins with me looking outside at a forest with all the trimmings: beautiful deer, wild rabbits, coyotes, pines. To me, completely stopping means that I open the curtains in the morning and stop, look, listen, hope, pray, laugh, but mostly listen for my own voice, the one I have distrusted for so many years. Completely stopping means to trust non-motion, non-activity, and non-thinking (almost). Using Incantation 1, I feel like I am going into myself or maybe that it's pulling me toward a place I have not been before. Fortunately, I have prepared for the last

*two years for this. I am ready to completely stop. I don't think
I was before."*

Maybe, unlike Jody, you haven't been preparing for two years to
completely stop. Maybe you are still at some great remove from
the possibility of completely stopping. Picture that "great
remove" as a physical distance between two objects, say between
two great oaks in a wooded pasture. In your mind's eye, picture
the distance between those two oaks shrinking. Let the earth
move and bring those oaks so close together that their branches
touch and become entwined. Feel how the distance between you
and your readiness to completely stop can also shrink, just by picturing it happening.

THERESA

*"Even though I don't hear it, I sense a clock ticking. I'm conscious
of what a precious commodity time is, so I'm always trying to conserve it, to hold onto it. I know that I'm doing some faulty thinking
here and I believe I wouldn't consider so much of my time 'wasted'
if only I could get centered. So I really will continue practicing
stopping . . . even though I sense that awful clock ticking."*

You can count seconds or you can let go of counting seconds. Which will it be? You can remain at the mercy of that unheard clock or you can banish it by completely stopping.

SUSAN

"I have fought long and hard with myself not to think of stopping as a negative. Stopping for me now is about surrendering, about being in the present and letting go of thoughts of the past and the future. It is also about being quiet, still, and inside my body. We spend so much of our day in a 'from the neck up' mode that it is both a shock and a joy to get back into the body. I think there really is something to the idea that we are spiritual beings trying to learn how to live in the physical body, rather than human beings trying to learn how to be spiritual. Stopping is a part of all of this."

Right now, turn "completely stopping" from a negative into a positive.

DEB

"I was recently sick for almost a month. Both Incantation 1 and being sick showed me what it means to come to a complete stop. My illness forced me to stop completely—I had no choice in the matter. What I noticed when I was getting better was that being

busy in my mind and wanting to be busy in my body 'came back.'
When I was too sick to move, I couldn't do anything and the sky
didn't fall. There was a total lack of monkey mind talk and
uncentered busyness. I remember thinking as I was getting better
how much energy that monkey-mind thinking cost me. The idea
came to me that perhaps if I wasn't that way when I was ill, I
didn't have to be that way when I was well. Incantation 1 gives
me the same message in the very first breath."

The sky won't fall if you completely stop for a few seconds. Find
the will to believe that. Return to Incantation 1, repeat it several
times, and experience completely stopping.

Chapter 5

Incantation 2: I Expect Nothing

While it is wonderful and necessary to have goals, dreams, hopes, and ambitions, it is a mental and emotional mistake to have expectations. Desire as much as you like. Plan as carefully as you like. Try as hard as you like. But expect nothing. If you expect nothing, you have a shot at centering. Use Incantation 2 to help you remember this vital detachment key.

Both reasonable expectations and unreasonable expectations uncenter us and bring us pain. Consider how unreasonable expectations affect us. If your mate was unhappy with you yesterday about your life choice to become an actor and is unhappy with you today about that choice, it is unreasonable to expect that he will be happy tomorrow. It is unreasonable to expect that he will be happy to hear that you did well at an audition or that you landed a coveted role in a play. It will only bring you pain to hope that he can share in your joy when you already know that he is unhappy with your choice and the way that you are defying him by pursuing your goals.

You could have a chat with him, on the off chance that in such a chat something important might get aired and inaugurate a change in his mind and heart. You could ignore him, you could leave him, you could reason with him, you could invite someone else to try to change his mind, and so on. But do not expect him to wake up one morning happy that you are an actor. To harbor that expectation is almost certain to bring you pain. You can't control how he feels, and wishing that you somehow could is unreasonable and completely uncentering.

What about reasonable expectations? Isn't it reasonable, for instance, to expect that it will be sunny on your beach vacation to a part of the world where the sun shines 340 days a year? Of course you don't control the weather, but as a statistical matter you should get sunshine. Why not go ahead and expect it, then? Because the universe does not owe you sun and is not obligated to provide you with sun. It may be reasonable to expect the sun to be shining when you arrive, but by harboring that "reasonable expectation" you are preparing yourself to have a negative emotional reaction to the quite natural event of occasional rain.

There is no one to be angry at and nothing to be sad about if you arrive and it is raining. If you are sad and angry that you are going to spend your measly annual vacation in the rain, that is more anger with the shape of your life and sadness about the shortness of your time off than it is a reaction to the rain. You needed the sun to be shining to justify the way you are living your life. That is what is typically true of our "reasonable expectations"—we attach to them for ulterior reasons. It is odd but true that we are trying to make our self-image secure by expecting the sun to be shining when we arrive on vacation.

It is better to let go of the idea that we can control anything, because as soon as we let go of our desire to control we become more honest and aware—and also more in control. By not attaching to even reasonable expectations we begin to force ourselves to live life in a more present way. The person who needed the sun to be shining will be sad the whole time. The person who can be present anywhere and is at peace with her life choices will walk on the beach in the rain and luxuriate as she strolls.

It is excellent and necessary to hold the intention to be an instrumental human being who makes her own meaning. At the same time, it is important to expect nothing. There is no paradox here. You decide to write an excellent novel—but you expect nothing. You decide to throw a ton of energy into your new business—but you expect nothing. You hope and pray that your new album will capture something of your recent joy and new musical ideas—but you expect nothing. You try your hardest at whatever you do, but you also surrender. Please do not move on until this distinction registers. By "expecting nothing" you are not "giving up." Far from it! You are making a decision to focus on what needs to be done rather than on outcomes.

Practice Incantation 2 right now. See if you can get its spirit and its meaning.

Though this discussion is necessarily brief, I hope that you can see why you would want to *empty yourself of expectations*. There is nothing to control, there is only your life to live according to your understanding of what principles you intend to manifest and what work you intend to attempt. You do not control your drinking; you honorably opt for moderation or sobriety. You do not control the course of your novel; you honorably work on your novel and both manage its direction and surrender to its logic. You do not control your children; you love them and help them. You do not control your mate, you do not control the flow of traffic as you make your way to work in the morning, you do not control your mother's stinginess or your father's temper. You give up the idea that you can control any of this and instead determine to live by your own cherished principles, doing the work that you have decided matters.

You empty yourself of expectations not in order to become a detached monk but in order to live the life you intend to live. Emptying ourselves of expectations is a graceful surrender to the facts of existence and a great release and relief. It brings with it

increased desire, increased energy, and increased presence. This is
what Incantation 2 can do for you.

> Practice Incantation 2 a few more times. Feel how
> exhaling "nothing" works. See if you don't experience
> a tremendous release.

Using Incantation 2

MARY

"Incantation 2 makes perfect sense to me. It reminds me of the mes-
sage of twelve step programs. I know that in the past I've been very
outcome driven: get the work done, get the A, get the new job with
more pay, get, get, get. One of the most difficult, yet necessary, things
I have learned in my thirties and early forties is that as much as I
delude myself, I really can't control outcomes. There are too many
variables: people, events, even the weather. And anyway, unexpected
things often happen as a result of the course I take toward a partic-
ular outcome. More often than not, it turns out that I don't want the
original results after all and something better happens. Emptying
myself of expectations means accepting that I can't make things hap-
pen the way I want. Most of the time, if I am patient and just go with
the flow, more interesting things happen than I would have ever envi-
sioned. It would be a parched life if only my own will were done."

How many variables affect every outcome? Have you ever stopped to make that calculation? If you did, you would know to try hard, so as to increase your odds . . . and also to expect nothing.

LESLIE

"I remember the time my first novel was soundly rejected by all the publishers to whom I submitted it. It appeared that I was a poor writer and that my work was just not acceptable. After grieving for two years, I chose to continue writing 'just for fun' with no thought of ever being published. I loosened up a lot and put together a book I worked on in an enjoyable manner. I never submitted it to a publisher; this time, a publisher came looking for me. Ever since, I have tried to write my books with the idea that if they are published, that's great, but if not, I am not worrying about it."

Can you really spend a year writing a book and then not care whether or not it's published? Yes, that's actually possible. You do everything you can to help find it a publisher and you also expect nothing. The first is right attachment, the second is right detachment. Take a few minutes and work out how you will master both right attachment and right detachment, since one is nothing without the other.

PAULA

"Something funny happened in the car yesterday. I had a series of errands to run around town. A CD I love, to which I was paying only slight attention, was playing. The day was sunny with a light breeze, the air smelled like lilacs, the trees and plants bloomed all along the avenue, and I had this feeling of settledness and contentment. I found myself taking in one deep breath and thinking (I expect) (nothing). As I breathed in slowly and out even more slowly, I was filled with this feeling of light bubbliness that made me very happy. It was one of those moments that are hard to explain to other people. But I would have to characterize it as joyful and relaxed, and I am attributing it, at least in part, to incorporating the ten-second centering incantations into my life."

Let Incantation 2 pop into your mind while you're driving, cooking, or mowing the lawn. Give yourself permission to think-and-breathe "I expect nothing" at random times, as a way to soothe yourself, detach, and center.

LORI

"It helped to think about why even 'reasonable expectations' are a problem. This is an idea I'd not heard before and it makes a lot of sense to me. 'You need the sun to be shining to justify the

*way you live your life' jumped right out at me and set off a chain
reaction of thoughts. It was truly an 'Aha! moment.' Likewise:
'There is only your life to live according to your understanding
of what principles you intend to manifest.' I know in my bones
that this is the way to go, yet it is incredibly difficult to carry
out. It seems impossible to put everything you have into something and still 'let go of the results.' This is so sane and true, yet
I guess that is my struggle; to live the way I know is right and
best for me to live."*

This is the essential struggle: to put everything into what you do
and to let go of the results nonetheless. You work incredibly hard
on your scientific research . . . and some lab publishes their results
first. You try to make the best widget possible . . . and an inferior
one with a snazzy name hits the marketplace before yours and
dooms your product. If you are practiced at expecting nothing, you
dramatically reduce your grieving time when such calamities hit.

BARBARA

*"I have a story right on point. A friend and I go to the seashore
every summer for five days, and of course we always pray for
good weather. One year it was forecast to be rainy the entire time,
but we made up our minds that we just didn't care and would find
some way of entertaining ourselves. Not only did we end up*

getting better weather than we expected, but we found new places and things to do and ended up having a wonderful time . . . much better than sitting around in the rental unit moping all day because it wasn't perfect beach weather every minute!"

That's it! That's the idea.

SANDY

"Recently I contacted someone I have been wanting to interview for quite a while. I sent out the request and promised myself I would not obsess, that I would just send the request and see what happened. I helped myself do this by using Incantation 2 several times. A day later he contacted me. I was thrilled. But more than that, I was happy that I hadn't agonized over whether he would respond or not and so was able to focus on other things. As I read the lessons about each step, the incantations become more meaningful to me. It's becoming less about practicing breathing-and-thinking and more about really understanding what centering means. I see that I've needed to learn this for a very long time."

Dream, but expect nothing. Desire, but expect nothing. Hope, but expect nothing. Release your need to control and gain real control.

Chapter Six

Incantation 3: I Am Doing My Work

Incantation 3 is the most interesting and intricate of the incantations. Each time you use it, you insert a new phrase that names some work that you hope to accomplish. There is great centering power in mindfully naming your work, as by naming it you at once fortify your intention and create a simple plan. Breathing-and-thinking (I am cleaning) (the closet), (I am writing) (my novel), or (I am paying) (the bills) has a calming effect even as it calls you to action.

The work you name can be the work you are about to undertake, like practicing your instrument or cleaning out the garage. You can also use Incantation 3 to announce an intention, for instance that you will write after work ("I am writing after work") or that you will clean out the closet when you get home from the supermarket ("I am cleaning when I get home"). You can also use it to work on a quality that you want to manifest, like courage or patience, or a state that you want to enter, like a calm, enthusiastic, or receptive state. For example, you might use (I am waiting) (patiently) at the dentist's office and (I feel open) (and receptive) upon entering a gallery of avant-garde paintings.

Incantation 3 can be used in an infinite variety of situations and possesses great flexibility. You might name your work in any of the following ways and in countless other ways as well:

(I am returning) (to my business plan)

(I am) (a real artist)

(I am working) (on my courage)

(Today) (I am calm)

(I accept myself) (completely)

(I will start) (my marketing)

(I am making) (that phone call)

(I am ready) (for that conversation)

(I will work harder) (than ever)

(I surrender) (to what is emerging)

The more accurately you name your work, the better results you will get from Incantation 3. For example, if you name work that you can't really support, like paying bills when you know that you're overdrawn, the outcome will not be a centered state. A certain honesty and awareness are needed in order for Incantation 3 to prove of use. You want to name your work truthfully and you also want to name it with clarity and exactness.

Let's say that you intend to make a difficult phone call to your mother, one in which you mean to tell her that she can't come to visit over the holidays. That's the work you plan to name using Incantation 3. The obvious phrase to incorporate is "I am calling my mother," or maybe, "I am making that difficult phone call." However, your real work might be to tell your mother what you're feeling or, conversely, to carefully hide what you're feeling. Or your work might be to stay calm as you speak or to stay strong in the face of her accusations and complaints. Therefore any one of the following phrases might be the one you actually choose to use:

(I will speak) (my truth)

–or–

(I will stay) (very calm)

–or–

(I won't reveal) (very much)

–or–

(I will stay) (strong)

Each of these phrases refers to the same task—calling your mother—but puts you in a different frame of mind and relates to a different intention.

Take your time and think through a variety of "name your work" situations. Look them over and practice Incantation 3 using different possibilities. The more you practice Incantation 3 and deepen your understanding of what "naming your work" means, the more value you'll find in using it.

Using Incantation 3

THERESA

"Incantation 3 places a greater burden on the individual than the other incantations, making it the most difficult incantation and also the most exciting one. At first, I found myself naming tasks that were far too daunting. I began to see that I set myself up for failure by doing this all the time. This afternoon, when I returned to my practice, I tried to name little 'bites' of something rather than the whole meal. I really like the 'bites' idea. I'm going to try to keep the work small, whether it's something I want to do or something I dread doing."

If the work you name is something impossible or just implausible, you won't center and you won't get your work done. If you set aside an afternoon and say (I am working) (in the garden), you will work calmly and productively. If instead you say (I am completely) (overhauling the garden), you're more likely to flee the house than get out your gardening gloves.

SANDY

"I think that naming your work is an essential step in order to gain clarity and have a precise vision of what you want to do. For me, I found it a bit difficult because I have a hard time narrowing things down and pinpointing one thing at a time to deal with. Today, it was about finding compelling people to interview for my show. First I used Incantation 2 to release expectations. Otherwise I would have approached 'naming my work' with too much fierceness—an 'I will accomplish this, damn it!' approach. By first releasing my expectations, I found myself growing calmer and more willing to focus on how I was going to get this done, as opposed to whether or not people were going to accept my interview request. Then I used (I am ready) (to call) for Incantation 3. And I felt ready! I made one call after another without procrastinating or feeling any stress at all."

This begins our look at how one incantation supports another. Sandy used Incantation 2, emptying herself of expectations, as a preliminary step to employing Incantation 3. In the space of half a minute she accomplished two important tasks: detaching from outcomes and announcing her intention to get on with her work. Not a bad use of half a minute!

KRISTEN

"I think it's important to put one's intentions 'out there.' It's also frightening; no more pussyfooting around. I've been using Incantation 3 to name my writing, my desire to stay calm, and my hope of recovering my creativity. I'm in the beginning stages of all three and need some self-encouragement. I can also see 'not letting people's opinions bug me so much' as work that I might want to consciously name, since I get very down after critique sessions at my writer's group. I'm not at all accustomed to carefully naming my work. In fact, I'm finding that I'm very squeamish. I'm afraid that instead of bringing me to my work, I'll get bombarded with all kinds of things that try to keep me from it. I guess I'm expecting the universe to teach me how to swim by tossing me into rough water, so I try to keep my intentions secret so that the universe can't torture me. It sounds silly, but there it is. Maybe one of the next things I'll name as my work is to get rid of these destructive expectations. I'm sure that they're holding me back."

The process of consciously naming your work may lead you to a self-exploration like Kristen's. You may find that you don't know what your work is, that you have so much work that you don't know where to start, or that you don't feel equal to any of your tasks. This process can provoke some anxiety! That's all right. If these are problems for you, you've been living with plenty of anxiety already. Trust that the way out is by going through: face your anxiety now, learn to name and do your work, and relief and calm will follow.

LORI

"I'm finding Incantation 3 excellent. It's very helpful to focus and make a conscious decision about what I intend to do next. It seems so much better than just spreading energy out there in scattershot fashion. Since I'm dealing with depression, anxiety, and now a possible medical threat, I choose (I am centered) (whole and strong). I'd like to name work like writing, journaling, calligraphy, poetry, or gardening, but right now I think I need to use this step more as a coping strategy. I've used other practices to help with my exhaustion and depression, but this is more specific and, I think, better."

The way Lori has made use of Incantation 3 is proof of the value of Ten Zen Seconds. By customizing Incantation 3 in a certain way, she has produced a powerful affirmation that supports her in her most important healing tasks. Naming your work is not just about getting the garage straightened out—it can also be about working to make yourself whole.

DEB

"The idea of naming my work stopped me at first. I didn't know what to say. Your suggestions really helped me put the words together. It also showed me how flexible I could be with the phrases I choose. I've tried 'I am rested and creative,' and, 'I am recovering my health and creativity.' I have been sick lately and need to get my rest and still create my art pieces. I've also tried 'I am calm and strong,' 'I can pace myself,' and 'I can be calm and creative.' At first it made me nervous to have to 'name work' that sounded so serious and difficult. Then I began to see that I could choose phrases that actually made it easier for me to get through the day."

Naming work is not the same as making work! It's a way to guide yourself calmly and peacefully through the day as you intentionally name how you want to feel and what you'd like to tackle.

MARY

"This process of naming work reminds me a little of a 'positive affirmations process' I went through a few years ago that involved consciously naming and refining a state of being or course of action that I wanted to undertake. I would tape the idea, complete with some sort of imagery, to the bathroom mirror, and while I brushed my teeth in the morning I would try to see myself in that situation or state of mind. But that technique didn't really take hold. So I've been spending far too much time

scurrying around paying no attention to my internal processes. It's good that I've started using ten-second centering and Incantation 3 especially. Recently I found myself working in a very difficult job situation. In retrospect I understand that the people were crazed and cruel, that the work was ill-defined, that the expectations were impossible, that the leadership was poor-to-nonexistent, and that I was drowning in that system. It's amazing how much more energy I have since I left that horrible place! So this is the perfect time to pay attention to naming work that I want to accomplish now that I am free of that environment."

Maybe your work is stressful or crazy-making. Then the work that you name when employing Incantation 3 might be (I am growing calm) (despite everything) or (I am looking) (for a new job). Incantation 3 isn't just for handling the next task on your to-do list. It's an integral part of the process of living the life you intend to lead and doing the work that supports that intention.

Chapter Seven

Incantation 4: I Trust My Resources

When you use Incantation 4 you announce to yourself that you have sufficient resources to achieve your goals and to successfully accomplish work of the sort that you named in Incantation 3. What would typically happen if you named your work and then said to yourself, "Okay, let's get on with it!"? As likely as not you'd immediately doubt that you were really equal to tackling the work you just named. You might even feel tempted to resume your fugitive flight away from centeredness. Incantation 4 is designed to help you believe that you are well-equipped to succeed.

The resources that you're trusting are internal, external, and even cosmic. Your internal resources include your brain power and heart power, your accumulated experience, your genetic wisdom, and the many qualities you possess but don't always manifest, like courage, passion, persistence, generosity, and strength. It is important that you believe that you possess these resources (and you do!) and important that you trust that they are available to you.

Your external resources include friends, advocates, and the accumulated wisdom of the species as stored in books, paintings, and music. They include the people you love, individuals currently unknown to you who might become important in your life, and groups and organizations that offer support. Your cosmic resources include the mysterious forces about which we know nothing and probably will never know anything. These are the dynamic forces at play in the universe that allow excellent novels to be born in flawed creatures, that permit us moments of peace and grace in a harried life, that darken the sky one minute and return the sun the next. Who knows which way the cosmic winds blow? In the face of this great mystery, why not opt to embrace the possibility of unfathomable cosmic resources?

The combination of internal, external, and cosmic resources that are at your disposal guarantee nothing. But they allow for the possibility that you can live in a principled, productive, creative, centered, and happy way. You will need luck; you will need to work hard; you will need to manifest the best in you and rein in the worst. "I trust my resources" is the succinct way of saying "I have a chance to do the work I intend to do and live the life I want to live—not a guarantee, of course, but a real chance."

If you deny that you have the resources to proceed, if you rush to dismiss rather than affirm your chances, you will not achieve a centered state. Even if you doubt that you possess these resources, optimistically announce that they are available to you by using Incantation 4. That way you will point yourself in the direction of possibility.

Using Incantation 4

SUSAN

"Usually I feel that I have sufficient internal resources. However, there are times when I lose this feeling, when I am overwhelmed by the process of daily living and lose my sense of the 'big picture.' Then I lose my connection to my resources. Incantation 4 has already helped me reestablish this connection and maintain it."

Picture yourself losing your connection to your resources. See this as a severed line to a life-giving air supply. Feel the panic well up in you as you realize that your air supply has been interrupted. Now calmly and magically heal the connection. Picture the hose line as completely whole again and feel the oxygen return to your lungs. This is how Incantation 4 works. It heals broken connections to the resources you possess.

ROSE

"As I strengthen myself, I seem to strengthen my external resources. By this I mean that as I gain confidence and experience I gain over- all strength and in turn my interactions with external resources strengthen. But there are too many times when I lament the fact that someone has more time, more money, or more opportunity than I do. I realize that getting stuck in jealousy not only diminishes my energy but darkens the big picture and keeps me stuck in place. I know that it's important not to compare but despite knowing this I struggle. Sometimes I get down and want to give up. I think, 'What's the use, I'm not important, and what I have to say is of lit- tle significance.' Incantation 4 is helping me with this, helping me believe that I have just as many resources as the people I envy."

Some people have more resources. Some people have fewer resources. So be it. The question is: do you have sufficient resources? Affirm that you do and grow centered. If you need more internal resources, affirm that as you grow centered, addi- tional internal resources will bubble up as if from an under- ground spring. If you need more external resources, affirm that you are equal to making new real-world connections. If you need more cosmic resources, surrender to mystery and see who or what responds to that invitation.

LORI

"I feel that I do have sufficient resources. The trick is remembering that fact when the chips are down. I'm much too inclined to look outside myself for answers rather than falling back on my own internal resources when nothing out there proves helpful. Using Incantation 4, I can consciously try to become more aware of what those resources are and remember times when those resources came through for me. It's really tough, though, if not impossible, to do this when you're depressed. It would have been a nearly overwhelming task throughout this past year. There were days when I clearly didn't care whether or not life continued. Life went on simply because I didn't know anything else but to keep moving."

Try using Incantation 4 when you're feeling down. It's hard to do anything when you feel depressed—that's the nature of depression. But ten seconds of breathing-and-thinking may be possible. Affirming that you trust your resources may loosen the grip of your negative thoughts and release your stored-up pain.

EMILY

"Cosmic resources have always been my deepest resources. But I forget this and forget how to access them when needed. I also underestimate how very much I need these cosmic resources and how deeply important they are to my life. Under certain kinds of

stress I am quick to devalue them and write them off as being 'airy-fairy' or part of my 'artsy/neurotic' personality. I forget my resources too easily, don't always have enough faith in them, and wait far too long to call on them. I hope that using Incantation 4 can help me remember."

Although you can't define your cosmic resources, try to define them anyway. Describe what you mean when you affirm, "I trust my cosmic resources." If you like your description, cherish it. If you can't come up with a description, well, that's the nature of mystery!

LYNETTE

"There have been times in the past when I doubted my resources, particularly when my strength and endurance were severely tested at my last job. But I have to say that now I have confidence—or at least growing confidence. I have discovered that I have often severely underestimated and underrated my internal resources. It took me quite a bit of counseling to understand how much of a survivor I really am and that I possess much courage, patience, perseverance, and strength."

Do you tend to underestimate your internal resources? Use Incantation 4 to remind yourself of your largeness.

JACKIE

"As I mature I've had to redefine the very idea of friendship. I used to have lots of friends, but they weren't real resources. They were more like energy drains. In the last two years I've lost more friends than ever before in my entire life; friends of the road, not of the heart. In the past year I've also gained more new friends than ever before and these are different kinds of friends: more accepting, more flexible, less dramatic, and less needy. They are people who just enjoy the company of my partner and me. I seem to be attracting happier, balanced folks. A lot of them have much to offer in terms of knowledge, advice, and encouragement without being pushy or controlling. For the first time in a long time, friends feel pleasant and rewarding instead of heavy and painful."

Not everybody you know is a resource. Use Incantation 4 to affirm, "I trust that I can tell which is a true resource and which isn't." One of the resources you possess is the ability to distinguish between apparent resources and real resources.

CHARLES

"As to my cosmic resources, I can't believe how often lately I've been saying, 'Just when I needed it, the universe sent me (fill in the blank).' I am writing a novel set in World Wars I and II, and over and over I have been sent information or knowledgeable people to

help. All I have to do is look up from my writing and voice a need, and it's amazing how fast a resource comes my way. Still, close attention has to be paid to this 'universe' that seems to be attending to me. The answer to the question I am asking isn't always as simple as a straightforward reply. Sometimes it seems that I am being led in a different direction than originally expected. So I keep trying to remain open and curious."

Pay close attention to how your resources operate. Sometimes they give you all the help you need and sometimes they only open a door through which you must still venture.

ALICE

"I believe that my internal resources are connected to a vast field of unlimited resources. Accessing these internal resources is the issue. Sometimes I can, sometimes it seems that I can't. Sometimes it's as if I have to pass by dragons or fierce guard dogs to get to them. For example, today as I began my artwork, I quickly discovered that I couldn't make my brush do what I hoped it would do. I had to stay with myself past a surge of dragon-thoughts like 'See, it was crazy to think you could do this' to get to my inner resources. Those resources guided me to deliberately paint a zigzag wiggly line, which I then recognized as far more meaningful than the straight line I'd planned to paint."

Do you have to get past a fierce guard dog of negativity and a dragon of doubt before you can trust that you have the resources you need? Picture yourself doing just that. Raise your hand and silence the guard dog. Raise your other hand and tame the dragon. Calmly walk by. Feel the ease of this and remember this feeling as part of your practice of Incantation 4.

BOB

"Twice today while practicing Incantation 4, very clear images popped into my mind. The first time I saw myself doing work in the past with ease and I had the clear sense that I could do that again. The second time I pictured the first small step I needed to take in my current work. I think that I'm beginning to own this incantation; it's taking hold."

Calmly invite in the realization that you have internal, external, and cosmic resources available to you. Feel the centering power of trusting in these resources.

---

incantation 5: I feel supported

You come to your parents and say, "I want to take a risky path and become a painter. I love art and don't want to do anything else. I know how hard a time I'm going to have, and I know that I may fall flat on my face. What do you think?" The answer that you want to hear is the very definition of "I feel supported." For one person it might be, "We'll help you through art school, and you'll always have a room in our house." For another person it might be, "Let's discuss the pros and cons, not to talk you out of it or to talk you into it, just to get our thoughts on the table." No one, however, would feel supported by the response, "You have no talent and you're a complete idiot!" or, "You're such a dreamer. Grow up already!"

There are many ways to interpret Incantation 5. You might think of it as, "I am capable and self-reliant and will do an excellent job of supporting myself on my journey." You might think of it as, "Maybe I didn't receive a lot of support as a child, but I feel supported by my friends, the universe, and my own inner strength." You might think of it as, "The people I'm about to interact with aren't my enemies, so let me deal with them in a genuine, open, friendly way." Use "I feel supported" as a centering reminder that you can support yourself, that others in your life are available to provide support, and that the people you meet may end up as your allies and advocates if you're open to that possibility.

What if you don't feel supported? Then use "I feel supported" as a classic affirmation, as a statement of a wish that you hope will come true. By using Incantation 5 this way, it helps counteract the sting of your current belief that you don't feel supported. It also points you in the direction of the way that you want to appear in the world, as a confident, competent person to whom good things happen.

Using Incantation 5

BEVERLY

"I hadn't thought much about a lack of support contributing to the difficulties I have as an artist. Yet I am aware that the support I receive from other artists contrasts with the lack of support I receive from my family, which is a sore point with me. If you don't feel supported by yourself or believe in yourself, all the

talent in the world will be wasted, and if you don't feel supported at least a little by other people, that does a lot of harm too. I'm using Incantation 5 to help me forget about my family's lack of support and to remind me about the support I do receive."

Incantation 5 can do double duty: It can help you forget painful memories of not being supported and acknowledge the support available to you right now. See if you can use Incantation 5 in a way that simultaneously serves both purposes.

ALEX

"As I don't feel supported, I didn't know what to make of this incantation. Was I just supposed to lie? Or was the idea like the idea behind affirmations, that something that isn't true might become true if you say it, believe it, and point yourself in that direction? But I tried it several times on different days, not knowing what to make of it and just to give it a chance. And I noticed something began to happen. I noticed that I was flooded by memories of those times, few and far between but still very real, when I did receive support. I'd managed to forget about them because of my general bitterness. So in a funny way Incantation 5 is helping drain me of my bitterness, which I knew I wanted to do but didn't know how to accomplish."

Use Incantation 5 even if you don't actually feel supported. You can't predict what interesting things will happen, but you can safely wager that something good will occur. Opt for trust and give Incantation 5 a try.

BARBARA

"When I started using Incantation 5, I naturally thought that I was saying something about what I wanted for myself. I wanted to feel supported, and I wanted to receive support. But after a few days a funny thing began to happen. I found that I was beginning to feel more supportive toward other people. I helped a woman at work whom I never would have helped previously. I agreed to contribute some time to a charity I respect. I went out of my way to do a small good deed for my aunt. I'm positive that all of this was a result of practicing Incantation 5. Maybe I was thinking 'If I give support, I'll get support,' but I don't think I was being that calculating. I think it was really coming from an altruistic and compassionate place. By saying 'I feel supported' I began to feel supported enough to begin to support others."

Feel supported and you will want to support others. Incantation 5 opens your heart and allows your bottled-up feelings of generosity out. In turn your generous actions will calm and center you.

JOHN

"I've always thought of myself as a lone wolf. Not as a self-sufficient lone wolf, like one of those mountain men who go to Alaska and live off the land, but more like a reclusive observer who comments on the culture and on human nature but who keeps those comments to himself. So I had the feeling that if I used Incantation 5 I'd only be summoning some aspect of self-support. In fact, that happened. Almost immediately I felt more confident about starting the Internet business I'd been hoping to start but hadn't managed to begin. But a second thing happened, too. I felt like I could invite in other people to help with the project and that they'd serve to support it, rather than prove some kind of impediment. I hadn't known it but I'd needed both things to happen: I'd needed self-encouragement and I'd also needed to let go a little of my lone-wolf persona."

The mountain man alone in the wilderness has made up his mind to live without the support of other human beings. The rest of us need an army of supporters: to bring food to our markets, to keep us connected to the Internet, to produce the books we write or the movies we make, to warm us when we are cold, and to encourage us when we are down. "I feel supported" also means "I accept that I require support" and "I am in it with the rest of the human race."

ALICE

"I'm one of those women who helps others and gives herself away. I can probably figure out all of the reasons for that, reasons that connect back to my rocky childhood, but that's the way it's been, and I've never been able to change that dynamic. I keep volunteering, I don't eat well or take care of myself, I let myself get too tired, I accept my husband's shortcomings—all the usual things that go with my personality type. Then the oddest thing happened when I started using Incantation 5. I started getting tougher. I could feel the difference. I started saying 'no' to things. Who would have thought that 'I feel supported' would translate as 'I won't take this crap any longer'? But it did!"

Feeling supported makes you stronger because it breeds confidence and calms and centers you. Use Incantation 5 to affirm that you feel supported and watch what happens!

BILL

"Recently I was invited to perform some short bits between acts in a variety show. The acts were master teachers at a variety entertainers' conference in Reno. Not only would I be performing with some of the great New Vaudevillians, but I would be doing so in front of my peers. The bits I meant to perform were either new or taken out of context from longer routines, so I felt

nervous on that score and also because this could be my big break. On the day of the show, I was in seminars all morning and then had to run to the drugstore to get some props. I arrived at the theater late. I didn't have time to do a proper warm-up, to review what I would be doing in the show, or to practice with the lights, curtain, and stage. These factors contributed to my nervousness, and I felt thrown off balance. I was not centered. On stage I found myself moving more than I needed to, rushing through the bits to get the uncomfortable performance over with, ignoring audience reactions, and messing up simple technical feats, like dropping a ball while doing a three ball juggle—and I've been juggling for over twenty years. I briefly broke character after that, and not in a funny way. In clowning, mistakes are part of the act, gifts even, that can set my creativity on fire. On this night they were just painful. Afterwards, some people did have nice things to say, but most of the conference attendees ignored me or avoided mentioning the performance. Watching parts of the video, the performance wasn't as bad as it felt, but there were long, uncomfortable moments that I cringe to think about. I looked like a deer caught in the headlights. Did I mention that there were talent scouts representing large international festivals in the audience? This performance was not my big break. I decided then and there to give ten-second centering an honest try. I was really tired of feeling uncentered and having these kinds of experiences.

I decided that I would use Incantations 1, 3, and 5 as a kind of package or sequence: 'I am completely stopping,' 'I am naming my work,' and 'I feel supported.' I figured that I could handle three phrases and that these were the ones that would help me get centered before a performance. So I began to practice them together. A few weeks later I had a pretty big performance lined up. The incantations had seemed to be working in practice but I wondered if they would hold up to a real performance. I couldn't predict if I'd actually use them and if they'd calm me down when my anxiety was flowing. I just didn't know. But when I got to the gig I found that I wanted to use the incantations. While I waited to go on I used my sequence, naming as my work 'I will perform beautifully.' I could tell that the incantations were working and that, in a funny way, it almost didn't matter what words I used. Just breathing that way and thinking that way were doing something profound to my system. I felt really stilled—the 'completely stopping' did that. I felt optimistic about what was about to happen. And I felt supported by these people who didn't know me and whom I didn't know. Somehow Incantation 5, tucked into my little sequence, had turned an anonymous audience into a roomful of friends."

Could you ask for greater dividends from an investment of thirty seconds in centering?

Chapter Nine

Incantation 6: I Embrace This Moment

Each of us is able to read a book, watch a television show, run errands, have a chat with a friend, and pass the time of day in countless other ways. But if we turn off the television set and just sit there, endeavoring to be present to what we really want to do next in life, we know how difficult that feels. Nor do we find it easy to encounter another person or our work in a present way. Uncenteredness causes us to pass the time of day busily and superficially.

The difference between passing the time of day and being present has to do with the nature of the commitment involved. If we're committed to our fugitive flight from meaning-making, we remain anxious and uncentered. If we commit to using our talents and resources in a serious, considered way, whether what we're doing is chatting with our daughter, writing our novel, or communing with nature, we fully inhabit the moment. Then we feel present and centered.

This is why *presence* is such a pregnant word and such a difficult state to achieve. It requires a special commitment. We have to find the courage to stop running, to risk quiet, to face our demons, and to treat life more seriously than we customarily do. When we become this quiet and this serious, we no longer allow distractions to bother us, we no longer lie to ourselves about our real tasks, and we no longer rush away from the present moment because a wave of anxiety has coursed through us. Presence, it turns out, is really a form of heroism.

When you are really present, having a chat with your mate, preparing a business presentation, or enjoying the night sky, anyone looking at you can tell that you are not on the run. They can tell that you are serious, even if you happen to be smiling or laughing. You may have thought that presence had something to do with "no mind" or "emptiness" and had detachment at its center. In fact, presence is a larger idea than that. To be present is to take your life as seriously as it ought to be taken as you bring your resources and your principles into the moment and intentionally make meaning.

Incantation 6 honors your commitment to personal meaning-making and reminds you that presence is an act of courage. When you "embrace now" you commit to an undistracted, authentic encounter with whatever is next in your life. When you breathe-and-think (I embrace)(this moment) you are choosing to encounter life in an aware way. Presence is the beautiful actualization of your potential; a centered, pregnant state full of the richness that is you.

Using Incantation 6

SUSAN

"I think that the difference between being present and not being present is one of awareness and connection. When I am fully present I am aware of myself in the moment and in my physical space. All my senses are engaged, and I am connected. Not being present for me is when I can't even remember what I just did. Presence equals stillness, activation of the senses, and a sense of self that spans the physical and the spiritual. Presence is about more than just growing quiet; first the mind becomes quiet, then the spirit becomes involved, then new power courses through you."

By employing the word *embrace*, Incantation 6 suggests love. Imagine that you are taking vows to love, honor, and cherish the present moment.

SANDY

"I have this deep-seated fear that the future will always mirror the past. I often find it hard to be in the present moment because I'm either trying to figure out what went wrong in the past so I can prevent it from happening again, or envisioning how past hurts might surface in the future. I'd never thought about being present as related to marshalling my resources. I like it! 'Growing quiet'

reminded me of the 'time-out' technique parents use with children—a technique that never appealed to me. But 'marshalling your resources' seems more like 'checking in with yourself,' an idea I do like."

Embracing the present moment is not a punishment, not a meditation where your feet go to sleep, your back aches, and the Zen Master whacks you with a stick if you don't sit up straight. It's the way you gather yourself so that you can manifest your full potential.

KRISTEN

"Being present means focusing on what I'm doing and filling myself up with the experience. It means losing track of time because time no longer matters. Being present carries no judgment; it's accepting what is, just because it is. There's no fighting the truth, no denial. Being present is sometimes like being plugged into an electrical outlet; currents that I've been dodging may strike with stinging force, but they're also bringing light to the dark places."

Kristen's is a beautiful image! When you embrace the present moment you allow your human electrical current to flow, showering you with sparks of illumination, filling you with energy, and, yes, sometimes shocking and stinging you with the truth. Picture yourself this still and this full of energy. When you embrace the present moment you grow centered and powerful and take the action you need to take without nagging doubts or wasted motion.

MARTY

"Embracing the present moment means something like devotion, I think, devotion to a cause, a feeling, a work of art, or a person, being there and working with all of your attention. Not being present means plowing through an entire meal without having tasted it, driving to a destination and not remembering the trip, being on 'autopilot,' doing one thing while thinking about the next hundred things to be done. Not being present means blocking my creativity because I'm so focused on things like, 'Will it make money? Will people like it? Will it save the world? Is it impressive? Does it validate my existence?' rather than on the act of creation itself. I am using Incantation 6 to change that. I find that if I repeat it a few times with my eyes closed, I come to my painting in an entirely different way, free of my usual anxious thoughts and ready for the encounter that is about to begin."

If you do the thing in front of you while thinking about the last thing you did or the next thing you have to do, you will not center.

If as you listen you only think about what you intend to say, you will not center. If you do not devote yourself to the present moment, you will not center.

LESLIE

"Mind chatter and an intense need to finish things and cross them off my list are my most immediate problems. Mind chatter is my biggest obstacle to becoming present. The difficulty of living 'in the process' and accepting that there will always be things undone while I'm alive make it hard for me to just stop and be. Plus, there is the rather substantial roadblock of being afraid that if I stop and look inside, I won't find anything there. I'm afraid that that's probably the real obstacle."

Are you afraid that if you embrace the present moment you will discover that you are empty, insubstantial, or ruined? You can't run fast enough to escape such fears. Use Incantation 4 ("I trust my resources") and Incantation 5 ("I feel supported") to steady yourself, and then use Incantation 6 to bravely face yourself in the moment.

BOB

"The difference between not being present and being present is the difference between caricaturing the world around me and painting it in artistic detail. I've had many performances where I rush

through them just to get them over with. I remember very little. When I'm present in performance, I may not slow down, but time seems to. It's like I discover a hidden world underneath. I'm aware of rich details without getting too caught up in them and I remember the experience from multiple points of view."

The present moment has an infinite richness to it. There are worlds above, worlds underneath, and worlds intertwined. If you've been running from the present moment because you fear that stopping would bore you, that you'd experience the present moment as empty and arid, change your mind. Use Incantation 6 to predict a kaleidoscopic experience rather than a static or stagnant one.

DEB

"I've never thought of presence as being about marshalling resources. That idea feels much better to me than the idea of just sitting still. One feels like an affirmative action and the other feels like being a victim. When I was little, being made to sit still and be quiet was a punishment for being bad. No wonder I get so twitchy sitting still! There was a phrase my mother used over and over again during my childhood and still uses: 'If I ever sit down, I'll never get up again.' As a child I took that to mean 'death' and as an older child I took it to mean that she'd be paralyzed if she stopped doing things. Both were scary thoughts that are probably still scaring me. How complicated 'stopping' and 'presence' are!"

Embracing the present moment is an affirmative action. It has nothing to do with sitting still and everything to do with bringing your heart, mind, and hands to the work you named in Incantation 3.

LYNETTE

"I find it important to acknowledge that not being present is a flight from making meaning, with anxiety as the underlying emotion. Stopping to acknowledge this and understanding that presence is a celebration are key steps toward fearless living. Just today I experienced the loss of a piece that is part of a larger sculpture that I've been working on for some time. I took the loss rather philosophically, considering how much I had invested in it. I think that using the Incantations has helped with this. I've become better at detaching from outcomes, better at feeling that things will work even if a given piece doesn't, and much better at staying in the moment without fear or anxiety.

Even if you embrace the present moment you will still make your share of mistakes and experience your share of failures. Embracing the present moment only guarantees that you will be centered and present, not that you will succeed. But by being centered and present you will succeed much more often!

THERESA

"While my husband is asking me a question, I'm thinking about the project I'm working on. When I'm working on the project, I'm thinking about the messy kitchen I left in order to work on the project. Even now, as I think about this question, I'm having to force myself not to think about the French homework I must do for a class I'm taking. I think the problem is mind chatter, but the mind chatter may stem from something deeper, perhaps a fear that if I stop moving, my life won't have meaning. Maybe it's something else. I really don't know. Can I move forward if I don't know what's causing my difficulties? I have to hope that I can. I have to convince myself to center and become present without worrying about knowing or not knowing the exact cause of things."

You may never know why exactly you find it hard to marshal your resources, embrace the present moment, and center. Just continue with your practice. Practice Incantation 6 and you'll find your way to presence.

Chapter Ten

incantation 7: I Am Free of the Past

Surely people are significantly harmed by experiences like being shamed, beaten, ignored, discounted, mocked, and abandoned. In addition, encountering a lot of disappointments, rejections, defeats, burst dreams, and unsuccessful outcomes cannot help a person feel sanguine about his chances or confident in his abilities. And mustn't the negative self-concepts that people form of themselves—for instance that they are unworthy, unlucky, incompetent, untalented, or undisciplined—regularly derail them?

While it is impossible to predict how nature and nurture will interact on a given child and impossible to know why a person has turned out the way he has, each has been sufficiently harmed in the past that the past is a problem for all of us. It manifests itself as bad memories that haunt us, as unhappy experiences that sap our confidence, and, most insidiously, as the mold that has pinched us into the skin we now inhabit. Our very personality is the problem. The harm done to us has become the person we are.

Incantation 7, "I am free of the past," is a wish and a demand. It means "I am ridding myself of bad memories," not because I have forgiven, forgotten, or surrendered, but because those memories weaken me and sting me to this day. It also means "I intend to be the person I want to be," that I am free of the past me who procrastinates, who takes wrong turns with a wink and a nod, who gives up too easily or doesn't get started.

Given that each of us has been harmed, what helps a person to heal? Love helps. What Carl Rogers called "unconditional positive regard" helps. Success helps. Support helps. Cognitive change helps; monitoring, confronting, and replacing our negative thoughts help. Behavioral change helps; doing even tiny things that move us in the right direction helps. Insight and awareness help; understanding how fear, worry, anxiety, and stress operate in our life helps. Hope helps. And Incantation 7 can help. Use it to heal the past and to set your present course.

When we remember that there are many ways to heal from the harm done to us, rather than one perfect one that keeps eluding us, we give ourselves options. If I say, "What should I do?" I am already making a kind of mistake, because embedded in that sentence is the idea that there is only one right thing to do. It would be better if we got into the habit of saying, "Of the many things I might do to help myself, which one shall I choose to do?" This is more cumbersome but it is also more helpful. You can reduce this phrase to the succinct "Which of many?" and let Incantation 7 stand for this idea as well. In addition to getting free of the past, you announce that you are open to healing from past wounds in any way that presents itself.

Using Incantation 7

JANE

"When I was about five I was enrolled in dance. My grandmother would take me. I loved it and felt I excelled at it, but it wasn't considered a stable endeavor by my grandmother, and my mother appeared to be disappointed that I wasn't good enough. I stopped dancing for two years, started again out of a desire to regain the happiness I used to experience, stopped again, started again, and finally stopped for good after getting too many messages from my family about not being pretty enough or talented enough. I stopped for decades until I just couldn't stand not dancing, which is when I took up folk dancing. But even after all those years I still kept hearing the old tapes and messages. I am not free of the past—but that's my work. I use Incantation 7 before I dance, because I find that I need to exorcise old demons that are trapped

in my body and that make me heavy and tired. I am only light when I have no past—it's a Zen thing, I think. I have all this training and body memory and only need to forget everything in order to dance beautifully. When I breathe-and-think (I am free)(of the past) I picture—and can feel—the demons leaving me, as if I were performing an exorcism."

Try out Incantation 7 and see if it feels helpful and congenial. If it doesn't, try using different language, as it may be the wording of the incantation and not its idea that is failing you. For instance, you might try (All that)(is behind me), (I am new)(each day), or (Right here)(right now), which is also a nice variation of Incantation 6, (I embrace)(this moment).

TOM

"My childhood was turbulent. My mother married four times and I went to sixteen different schools before graduating high school. Mother had six kids, three of whom died at birth. My natural father was a horror; evidently an abusive man, but I can't remember him in any detail. He left when I was ten, at which time I stopped having fainting spells and bad headaches. Mother remarried when I was thirteen to an ineffectual man, sweet though he was. She forever confided in me, quite inappropriately, her sexual frustrations with him. She divorced him after a few years and subsequently married

two more men, one an alcoholic and the last a nice man who soon died from Parkinson's Disease. Tennessee Williams couldn't have written a better scenario than my childhood. Now, working in a pressure-filled, high-tech job, I find that the past intrudes in strange ways that are doubly disturbing because they come on so suddenly. I'll be running a meeting and right in the middle of the meeting I'll have a flashback memory of my mother sitting on my bed carrying on an inappropriate conversation. I've found that I can use Incantation 7 right there, on the spot, without closing my eyes and without drawing attention to myself, to get that whole Tennessee Williams thing out of the room. Thank God for that!"

The beauty of ten-second centering is that you can use it in real-life situations, when you need to center the most. Once you practice the technique and acquire your repertoire of incantations, you'll know how to center when the past intrudes and when an uncentering situation arises.

ANNE

"My problem may sound odd. When I was a junior in college I won a pretty prestigious national short story competition. Naturally that made me feel proud, but I found that almost as soon as I got the news of that award I started having real trouble writing. I would start a short story, write maybe three lines, reread those three lines

with disgust, throw the story away, and not write for a week or maybe a month—and then for much longer stretches, until I wasn't writing at all. I did technical writing during the day and blamed my inability to write stories on the fact that I was writing all those boring manuals and that I was burned out on writing by the time I got home. But I never really believed my own excuses. Finally it dawned on me that, as a lifelong perfectionist, that award had put me over some kind of edge and caused me to trash every new story without giving it a real chance. I was saying things like, 'An award-winning writer would never write that,' and, 'I can't follow up my award-winning story with drivel like that,' without knowing that I was saying anything of the kind. I only realized that I'd been saying those paralyzing things when I encountered Incantation 7 and realized that what was burdening me the most from my past was my one success—or rather the way that one success had exacerbated my fears and doubts about my basic worth. So I thought I would give 'I am free of that story' a try. And it worked! I've returned to writing, and now when I feel that a story isn't good enough I take a deep breath, get myself centered, remind myself that writing is a process and that I have to let the process unfold, and finish up with 'I am free of that story.' That poor story! As if it were ever to blame! But as innocent as it is, I have to put it behind me to free myself of the sense that I can never succeed again."

The goal of Incantation 7 is to help you free yourself from the past, even if the past event you are trying to get free of was a positive one. Our successes can burden us just as heavily as can our failures, and our goal is to rid ourselves of anything, positive or negative, that sits like an albatross on our shoulder and makes our current journey more difficult.

MARK

"I bet my problem is very common. If I don't manage to say the right thing to someone, if I get into some kind of edgy interaction with someone at work, if I do something one way and then wish I had done it another way, I obsess about what just happened all day long. I can't get the event out of my head, which of course makes what I'm currently doing go more poorly, giving me even more to brood about. It turns out that my problematic 'past' is what happened just five minutes ago, something that someone said to me or that I said to someone, and keeping that past alive in my head is just about the biggest problem I face. I am always brooding about what just happened, which means that I am never really present, never calm, and never living up to my potential. That's why Incantation 7 struck me as so important to master. I began using it whenever I noticed myself brooding about something that had just happened. But the language didn't seem quite right, as 'past' seemed to signify events from twenty years ago and

not twenty seconds ago. So I changed the incantation to 'I am let-
ting that go,' which felt exactly right. For me, 'I am letting that go'
puts the past in its proper place—that it is in my control and
already behind me. If I want to keep something from the past
alive, I can, and if I don't, I can get rid of it in ten seconds flat."

The "past" that is currently troubling you may be the very recent
past: something that happened yesterday evening, an hour ago, or
even a minute ago. Something from a minute ago is already in the
distant past—unless you can't free yourself from its grip. To rid
yourself of the recent past, you might try one or another of the
following variations on "I am free of the past": "I am free of
that," "That isn't worth holding," or "I am done with that."

Chapter Eleven

Incantation 8: I Make My Meaning

Centering and meaning are connected. If your days don't feel meaningful then an uncentering restlessness and boredom set in, along with existential anxiety and, eventually, depression. Incantation 8 can prove a great help to you in this regard, because it reminds you of meaning's central secret, that it is a thing to be made and not found. The metaphor of "seeking meaning" is outdated and no longer viable. There is only the meaning we make.

Meaning is more like a choice than a lost object. You don't write a novel to find meaning, you write a novel because it feels meaningful to write a novel. You don't marry to find meaning, you marry because it feels meaningful to love and to live with this particular person. You don't give to a charity because you hope that by giving you will find meaning, you give because you believe in what the charity represents. Until you make such meaningful investments, no meaning exists.

Many people today suffer from meaning problems. They've gotten a whiff of meaninglessness and don't know where to turn to find meaning. The existential psychotherapist Irvin Yalom used the following anonymous suicide note as an epigraph on the experience of meaninglessness in *Existential Psychotherapy*. The despairing suicidal person wrote:

> *Imagine a happy group of morons who are engaged in work. They are carrying bricks in an open field. As soon as they've stacked all the bricks at one end of the field, they proceed to transport them to the opposite end. This continues without stop. Every day of every year they are busy doing the same thing. One day one of the morons stops long enough to ask himself what he is doing. He wonders what purpose there is in carrying the bricks. And from that instant on he is not quite as content with his occupation as he had been before. I am the moron who wonders why he is carrying the bricks.*

This visceral experience of meaninglessness causes a person to need good reasons to go on, reasons that can counteract, by their excellence, the felt experience of meaninglessness. If those good reasons can't be found, a meaning crisis occurs. How many people have encountered this visceral experience of meaninglessness? Several years ago Viktor Frankl, like Yalom a meaning-oriented psychotherapist, provided some suggestive numbers. In one study, he reported an incidence rate for "existential vacuum" of 81 percent for American college students. In Yalom's own investigations, he found that 30 percent of the subjects in one of his studies had "some major problem involving meaning." Who today hasn't gotten a significant whiff of meaninglessness?

You counteract this experience of existential vacuum, this whiff of meaninglessness, and these meaning problems by deciding that you will invest meaning somewhere and by then investing it. You make a decision to care. You make a decision to be passionate. You make a decision that this relationship matters or that that work matters. Does it matter to Martians or to Venutians? No. But you decide that it matters to you, that according to your understanding of how your life is to be lived this is a meaningful relationship to cultivate or a meaningful job to undertake.

Human beings always had the potential to know meaninglessness. Our modern times activated that potential. We call this the modern period because of profound changes wrought on the species by increased scientific understanding, paradigm shifts in the way we view the universe, and progress in the direction of an enlightened regard for the individual. It's not even mildly strange that advancements in scientific understanding and a heightened valuation of the individual have provoked a culture-wide explosion of meaninglessness. You can't peer behind the curtain and spot the cogs and wheels, you can't inflate the individual and give him outlandish hope while leaving him life-sized and all-too-human, and not create an epidemic of meaninglessness.

As simple as Incantation 8 is, it can counteract all of this. It is a complete existential cure. If you are a believer, you must still make your meaning, as no religion posits that it is the business of gods to announce to you whether it is more meaningful to become a doctor or a lawyer, for instance, or to live in Boise or Boston. You use Incantation 8 to remind yourself that you can only serve your god or your spiritual nature by deciding where meaning must be invested. If you are not a believer, you have an even clearer mandate, as there is nothing and no one to tell you how to live or why to live. Either you make your own meaning or you get swallowed up by meaninglessness.

You can construe Incantation 8 as a short, sweet chat that you regularly have with yourself about your existential responsibilities. Indeed, all the incantations have a hidden existential component, which helps explain why they possess their power. For instance Incantation 1, "I am completely stopping," really translates as, "Even though I'm afraid that I may encounter a whiff of cosmic meaninglessness if I stop completely, I nevertheless know that I must stop to center and I courageously will stop." Incantation 6, "I embrace this moment," really translates as, "I don't have to worry about past meaning losses or future meaning crises. I can make meaning by being present right now." Each incantation hints at the proactive existential work we must do if we modern people are to center.

Likewise Incantation 3, "I am doing my work," can be used to name existential work and to support your use of Incantation 8. Consider trying out some of the following as Incantation 3 phrases that affirm your heroic decision to make meaning and to matter:

(What I do) (matters)

(I take) (responsibility)

(My life) (has value)

(I am committed) (to caring)

(Passion creates) (meaning)

(A path) (with heart)

(Life is in) (the living)

These ideas about making meaning may be new to you. Think about them a bit and, better still, just start using Incantation 8. Use it to center when you feel at sea and don't know what to do next. Use it when you want to put your passion and energy somewhere but don't know where to turn. Use it when you feel blocked and uncreative. Use it when you feel bored, restless, or depressed. It is a key to centering—and a key to a great deal more.

Using Incantation 8

MARTHA

"I have experienced meaninglessness most of my life. I always thought it was simply 'depression' and had no idea that it could be

'more' than depression or 'other than' depression. Meaninglessness is soul-destroying and deadening and sucks the life right out of you. It literally feels like 'nothing matters' and 'there's no good reason to live' and 'why bother?' And it's all the more exquisitely painful because no one else in my environment ever seems to feel that way—or rather, those who do (usually women) are written off by everyone (including myself) as 'hysterics' and 'neurotics' not worth bothering with. I am just thrilled to have this new frame, that I must make meaning, and that I can stop waiting for some miracle of meaning to happen! I am using Incantation 8 all the time now, even to 'invest meaning' in doing the laundry or making a pot of soup. It makes all the difference in the world."

If you've had problems with meaning, that makes you a full-fledged modernist, not a neurotic or a hysteric. As a full-fledged modernist you have no option but to announce what meaning you intend to make, believe in your own choices, and make that meaning. Support your intentions by using Incantation 8.

KATHY

"I experienced severe meaninglessness several years ago and wonder whether it will surface to that degree again in my life. I remember describing to someone how I could not see color at that time in my life. It wasn't that I couldn't actually see it, but rather that the impact

of color didn't reach me. Since those bleak months I've experienced lesser bouts of the same meaninglessness or variations on it. My experience is that of lethargy, tearfulness, and anhedonia—the inability to experience pleasure. Sometimes it has been related to stressful jobs and sometimes the symptoms seem to appear randomly. To combat these feelings I do several different things. For one, I take antidepressants. I feel that these have been effective insofar as they provide a space or distance between the despair, lethargy, or emptiness that seem to be the symptoms that I experience. What I feel has been even more effective are my efforts to create a flexible, relatively well-paying work life. I've determined that flexibility in schedule and location makes me feel much less hemmed in and much less of a cog in the machine. I have that part worked out relatively well now. But I see that there is more to do. More and more I find myself noticing when I'm not centered and taking the time not only to look for my center again, but also to notice what physical and emotional sensations go with feeling uncentered. All of this is part of my process of making my own meaning. I never knew how much that task rested squarely on my shoulders, but whether it's 'just' being or actively doing, I need to bring conscious awareness with me in order for meaning to exist. Incantation 8 is helping me do just that."

Maybe you've experienced depression. Maybe you take medication to fight your depression. Try Incantation 8 too. If your depression happens to be caused by your problems with meaning, Incantation 8 may prove a useful antidepressant and even a complete cure.

SUSAN

"I see two ways that meaninglessness affects my life and the lives of the people around me. One relates to our industrial, production-oriented, consumer culture. We work to produce money and in doing so, like the morons with their bricks, we wonder what we are doing. Then our consumerist economic climate gives us a solution: buy, buy, buy. We're told that's the solution to our problem. Sooner or later, though, we find out that it's not. The other form of meaninglessness comes as part of the natural cycle of creating. I have witnessed in myself that the 'winter' before 'spring' or the nothingness before new beginnings is a time where I feel the absence of meaning. It's this meaning crisis that drives me to create something meaningful. I move ahead with the process of creating a new piece, forging a new outlet, finding a new technique, or trying a new class. Although I might not recognize the meaning immediately, I feel it and it feeds me the 'meaning' nutrient I need. I think that the most important thing for me to realize is that meaninglessness is not a feeling that is wrong. I don't need to combat it, heal it, or fear it. It only needs to be acknowledged, lived with, and listened to. It always has something to tell

me, and although it may slow me down and frustrate me, I know that it's essential. And in dealing with all of this, I think that the incantations are wonderful tools. They help me sit still and listen and feel less fearful of the nothingness before creation, less fearful of the blank canvas before the painting."

Feel proud that you have stepped to the plate as a meaning-maker. Use Incantation 8 to steady your resolve and to help remind yourself that meaning-making is not only your duty but a golden opportunity to choose work that you love and the life that you want to lead.

Chapter Twelve

incantation 9: i am open to joy

Joy is the word we use for a deep, delicious feeling that sometimes arises in us just because the sun is shining and it feels good
to be alive. But because of our frenetic pace, our worried mind,
our existential difficulties, and our culture's injunctions against
ecstatic experience, joy is in remarkably short supply. How many
times a day do you experience joy? Probably very few—and
maybe even none. How often do the people around you look joy-
ously transported? Seldom, I'll bet—and maybe even never.

An absence of joy is uncentering. Joy quells anxiety, dispels sadness,
and promotes optimism. When we are less anxious, less sad, and more
optimistic we are naturally more centered. Picture yourself smiling,
happy, enjoying yourself, and in an excellent frame of mind. Isn't that
the image of a centered person? Now picture yourself rushing, your
forehead wrinkled, a frown on your face, a weight on your chest. How

centered do you look in that picture? Isn't that image the epitome of uncentered living?

We could have a tea party with our child and feel joy; but instead we worry about our child's grades and the laundry waiting. We could pull an art book off the shelf and feel joy; but that seems like such an indulgence, given all the errands we have to run. We could bake bread and feel joy; but first we'd have to wrestle with a hundred issues about calories, sugar, and carbs. Our mind makes worries and shuts the door on joy. How can we pry the door back open?

We open the door by using Incantation 9. Incantation 9 reminds you that joy is available to you, that you are on the side of joy, and that joy is permitted even in a fast-paced, task-driven, no-nonsense culture. You can use Incantation 9 in conjunction with Incantation 3, the name-your-work incantation, to create a powerful twenty-second invitation to joy. You might use an Incantation 3 phrase like the following to accompany Incantation 9:

(I will take) (a long walk) and (I am open) (to joy)

(I will commune) (with art) and (I am open) (to joy)

(I will get) (a little sun) and (I am open) (to joy)

(This meeting) (will go well) and (I am open) (to joy)

(Ten minutes of) (pure relaxation) and (I am open) (to joy)

(I will write) (during lunch) and (I am open) (to joy)

(A special dinner) (with Bill) and (I am open) (to joy)

Suggesting that we might find some joy in our lunch hour or our next meeting is hardly a habit that most of us cultivate. Because we don't cultivate that habit, because we rarely announce to ourselves that we're on the lookout for joy, we miss opportunities to experience joy and we miss the centering advantages of feeling good. Give Incantation 9 a try right now and start to lobby for more joy in your life.

Using Incantation 9

SANDI

"I used to mistrust my feelings of joy and kept my nose to the grindstone. Expecting the worst was what I was taught both at home and at school. It wasn't until college that someone pointed out that the faith I was brought up in could be joyful, the service a celebration. I thought they were nuts. I was brought up to believe that work was just that—hard, difficult, and joyless. And this belief system creeps in and under and around all of my experiences. I can see that I have a real fear of joy. I fear that if I let myself feel it, nothing will ever be the same. And what if that feeling goes away? Won't that be worse than not feeling joy at all? But I'm trying to use Incantation 9 to support the idea that joy is a good thing. I've also put words like play, enjoy, and happy into my 'work naming' statement. Still, I keep feeling like I'm cheating and that I'm going to get caught. Those old beliefs are so hard to get rid of!"

Were you brought up to believe that life had to be hard and work joyless, and that even your religion demanded duty, not celebration? Erase those tapes right now. Picture yourself running a high-tech machine whose only function is to erase the idea that joy is impermissible. Turn the machine on. Feel it warm up. Hear it begin to whir. Experience joy well up within you.

VANESSA

"It seems that emotionally I think that too much joy can lead to sadness. Intellectually I know that's not true, but it's a tough feeling to overcome. I suspect that part of the reason has to do with my Scandinavian maternal grandmother. She was a strong influence on my mother, who was an equally strong influence on me. There's an old Scandinavian saying: 'Laugh before supper, cry before bedtime.' Too much joy is just a bit frightening, I guess, especially if your culture trains you as a child to be scared of it. The other reason I've always felt that joy can lead to sadness is the fear that if things are going too well—look out! That fear permeates our society. I suspect that our Puritan forebears are still exercising their influence over us in this regard. So I am using Incantation 9 as a reminder of the many joys available to me, if only I can pay attention to them, if only I can sidestep my upbringing and this Puritan culture. Then something that we never consider a joy—a weed, for instance—might have its joyful side. I might be able to see it as a lovely purple flower!"

You may have to sidestep your culture in order to experience the centering influence of joy. Picture yourself literally sidestepping your culture as if it were a pothole on your path. People are rushing—you sidestep their energy. People are frowning—you sidestep their mind-set. Feel as if you are dancing a culture-sidestepping jig.

TONI

"I go back and forth on joy. Sometimes I feel like it's our birthright. Other times I feel like it's too much to expect. Still, I make it my business to try to smell the roses along the way, even if I have to be prudent in how I share that experience with others. I remember one time when my friends and I were in a casino; we yelled with joy when we won fifty cents. The woman at the machine next to us glared at us like we were her worst enemy. I've even heard people say that it's not appropriate to love a friend; only families should have that honor and friends should simply be liked. Yeesh! What are people thinking?"

Maybe you will need to be prudent about when, where, and how you share your joy. Or maybe you can become an ambassador for joy! Either way, experience joy and shed the negative thoughts and feelings that uncenter you.

ALLEN

"How Incantation 9 works for me depends on how it's used or worded. For example, I tried using 'Creating is a joy' instead of 'I am open to joy' and that felt like a flat-out lie. That statement isn't true for me at this point in time. However, 'It's okay to feel joy' worked well for me. It's more a matter of giving myself permission, of opening a door to possibility, rather than trying to bluntly convince myself that I'm feeling something that I'm not. That also helps me switch my focus from the cloud to the silver lining in life, to what I want as opposed to how I actually feel."

Incantation 9 may not bring you instant joy. It may only point you in the right direction. That "only" is not to be sneezed at.

MONICA

"To my mind joy doesn't arrive 'in your face' in a way that can't be ignored. Rather it's small and quiet and extremely easy to overlook. It also seems related to gratitude and appreciation. I've heard that's why 'gratitude journals' and thanking exercises are so successful, because they involve a deliberate attempt to look more closely and name the things in everyday life that you can be grateful for. I think that joy springs from that type of mind-set. So I am trying to use Incantation 9 not only to remind me to be open to joy, but also to remind me to be thankful for what life has to offer and appreciative of what I have."

What if joy is sometimes small and quiet? Then you will have to grow still to not miss it. Use Incantation 1 ("I am completely stopping") and Incantation 6 ("I embrace this moment") to steady yourself before inviting joy in. In this way you will have created a three-incantation, thirty-second sequence perfect for bringing small joys to your attention.

KAREN

"Everyone knows the experience of wanting something, imagining the joy that having it would bring, only to finally get it and then watch it become part of the vast mass of taken-for-granted-ness in our lives. Whether it's love, some object, or some achievement, everything fades in joyousness the more you come to expect its presence. So it struck me that I could experience more joy if I connected it up with Incantation 2 and the idea of letting go of outcomes and expectations. And that works beautifully! By creating a world of expectations before we begin, we set ourselves up for joylessness when things don't work out as planned or even if they come true perfectly. When I use the two incantations together, first expecting nothing and then opening to joy, I find that I get surprised by life, and by how much love is in my life, by how beautiful the world can look. I haven't felt that sense of surprise in a long time."

Look at the twelve incantations again. See how you might connect each of the other eleven with Incantation 9, using it either before it or after it. With some, the connection may seem strong and sensible. With others, the connection may seem forced and unworkable. This exercise will give you a beginning sense of how to marry incantations, how to choose among them, and how several may be built into a personal Centering Sequence.

TAMARA

"I'm not particularly suspicious of joy. I seek it and find it regularly. Joyful experiences and attitudes are frequent in my life and I see how they contribute to my contentment and peace. But there is a deeper level of joy that I aspire to, a more intense experience at a core level, less to do with experiences and events than with being. Am I talking about existential joy? Very possibly! I'm not suspicious of it, either. I just haven't been able to find that place within myself for extended periods of time. Sometimes months and even years go by without my experiencing joy at that level. I can see that being centered has many, many layers. To experience joy as a result of doing is to be on the right path, and that's a good thing. But to be in that centered place from which joy radiates, to be joy, is even more wonderful and enticing."

Who knows where an openness to joy may lead? Maybe it will lead to moments of joy and a steadier center. Maybe it will lead to a way of life full of surprise, wonder, and contentment.

Chapter Thirteen

Incantation 10:
I am equal to this challenge

We regularly get uncentered in anticipation of doing something that strikes us as hard to do. The thought of that unpleasant task raises our anxiety level, which immediately uncenters us. For many of us, an awful lot of tasks feel hard to do, whether it's straightening out the garage, talking to our children about their school performance, staying married to our spouse, or getting up to go to work. The more that the things we do feel like a strain and heavy lifting, the more uncentered we remain.

Think of one of these hard-feeling tasks. Bring it to mind as calmly as you can, which is no easy feat since thinking about it will raise your anxiety level. Get it clearly named: "I need to clean out the hall closet"; "I need to have a chat with Johnny about his weight"; "I need to tell Mary at work that I'm tired of pulling all the overtime." Follow that thought with Incantation 10, breathing-and-thinking (I am equal) (to this challenge). Repeat the process of naming the task and following it with Incantation 10 until you have the visceral sensation that you really are equal to confronting this challenge.

Experiment with Incantation 10 today, using it to tackle one of the hard things in your life. First, bring the hard task to mind. Then announce to yourself when you mean to tackle it: for instance, "I'm going to have that chat with Johnny about his eating habits as soon as he gets home from school and before he hits the refrigerator." As that moment draws near, use Incantation 10 or one of the other incantations (for instance, "I trust my resources," "I feel supported," or, "Talking to Johnny is my work") to keep yourself centered. Then, when you hear Johnny arrive home from school, use Incantation 1 ("I am completely stopping") to quiet your racing mind and Incantation 10 ("I am equal to this challenge") to marshal your strength.

When might you use Incantation 10? Whenever an upcoming task feels hard or whenever you want to tackle something that you've been avoiding. Maybe there's a business call that you haven't felt equal to making. The next time the thought of making that call pops into your head, don't swipe it away or push it back down. Turn to Incantation 10. Breathe-and-think "I feel equal to this challenge." The odds are that you will. Bring something that you've been procrastinating about to mind right now and see if Incantation 10 can help you move forward with renewed strength and courage.

Using Incantation 10

JEAN

"I had a task that was shouting to be used in this experiment. It wasn't something that was terribly hard or that would over-tax me in any way, it was just a program I had to develop for our computer techies to turn into a database for me. I'd been putting it off for at least a week. Each time I picked up the stack of paperwork, I was both bored and irritated that it had to be done and I allowed other things to quickly distract me. But this time just thinking about having Incantation 10 avail-able convinced me that I'd be able to get through the task easily. I chose to name an hour the following morning when I would commit to calmly accomplishing it. Instant relief. There was no nagging guilt to take home, because I knew it would get done. I found that I didn't have to think about it all during the evening. The following morning I gave Incantation 10 a try and actually got the work done an hour earlier than I'd planned. I was simply ready to tackle it. Obviously the 'real' work was in my attitude, not in the task. It felt peaceful, easy, and natural. How many problems of this sort might actually be just this easy to handle?"

Aren't most tasks "easy" or "hard" depending solely on our attitude? Why do we wait so long to replace the light bulb in the garage or tell our mate what's bothering us? We wait so long because our mind has gotten in the way. Use Incantation 10 to wrest back control of your mind and to begin the process of reframing tasks as doable rather than difficult.

LESLIE

"Clearing my work space was the task I chose. I really need a clear, uncluttered work area, not covered with piles of things that have to be done before I can do anything else. I didn't feel particularly calm thinking about this task, because I've tried to clear my desk so often, but I used Incantation 10, repeating it a few times, and discovered that I was determined to get the job done. I set my mind to it and didn't do anything else until I finished. It was a thrill to see my workspace free of clutter. There is more to be cleared in the rest of the room, but I know that I can get it done. It's reassuring to know that I have these incantations as a resource to help accomplish other things that I want to do."

Focus on the thrill of accomplishment, not on the difficulty of the task. Name as your work (I will be thrilled) (to be done) and pair it with Incantation 10 to produce a powerful twenty-second motivational tool.

SUSAN

"I tried three hard tasks: confronting an unwanted task at work, facing a busybody neighbor on the way home, and opening a letter containing a critique of my first story in a writing course. I chose the work task because it was the most immediate. I chose the neighbor because I was spending way too much time dreading going home on account of this man. I chose the letter as soon as I opened the mailbox and saw it there. I'd been nervous about receiving it, so it was a natural choice. I was skeptical at first that Incantation 10 would help with any of this, especially when it didn't seem to make the first task that much easier. I think that when the task is simply boring or I'm feeling lazy, maybe Incantation 10 won't work that well for me. But it proved really useful on the second task. I repeated Incantation 10 all the way home and when I got to my house I used Incantation 3 and breathed-and-thought 'John does not run my life.' That felt really good. The best time was before opening the letter. By the time I got through Incantation 10 two or three times, I was actually looking forward to opening the letter and even rushed the incantation the last time in order to tear the envelope open. Sometimes all the positive self-talk, deep breathing, and meditating in the world have no effect on me if my anxiety level is off the scale. However, for tasks that are difficult but still manageable I can see Incantation 10 definitely helping."

Maybe sometimes you'll feel too anxious and Incantation 10 alone won't do the trick. Maybe sometimes the task will be off-the-chart hard and you won't be equal to the challenge. It's easy to imagine situations where Incantation 10 doesn't solve everything. But if it only works three times out of ten or five times out of ten, isn't that already a small miracle?

TINA

"I decided to work on a project that I'd let sit too long. My goal was to 'finish it' but I realized that putting that pressure on myself is what leads me to let it sit and that my sculptures always take longer to finish than I seem to realize. I wish I could remember that whatever time it takes is simply part of the process. I focus too much on being productive and end up feeling guilty, stressed out, and paralyzed. At first several tasks came to mind, in fact far too many. I narrowed them down to three tasks and then decided that I had better focus on just one. That alone helped! I used Incantation 10, managed to work on the sculpture, and actually got closer to finishing it. I can see how, if I let it, Incantation 10 can help me focus on one task at a time instead of weighing myself down with too many tasks all at once."

Let "I am equal to this challenge" stand for "I am equal to this challenge and I am focusing on it, not on it and eighty-three other challenges as well." Use Incantation 10 to encourage yourself and also to focus laser-like on the task at hand.

GERRY

"I chose to tackle editing my book of short stories, which I've been putting off for eight weeks. My editor is waiting for the revisions. It needs to be done! Actually, a number of tasks came to mind, but this is the most pressing and probably also the most complicated. But with the incantations as a resource I felt calm and determined. They helped me focus and realize that, since I must do this editing, I might as well relax and concentrate on it. I've just started the process, and it's going to take days! But Incantation 10 has been very helpful, and I'm positive it will continue to be a blessing as I work to complete the revision."

Many tasks don't get done in the blink of an eye. They may take hours, days, weeks, months, or years. You may need to use Incantation 10 a thousand times during the course of writing your novel or getting your business up and running. Do just that. It is ready and waiting.

GEORGINA

"I chose as my hard task continuing to work on a wooden box that I've been making. It's something that I want to get done. Many tasks came to mind but this one is a priority right now. I did feel calmer knowing that I had the incantations as a resource, but unfortunately it was one of those days that got clean away from me and I never found a convenient time to really give it a shot. So, except for some preliminary work, I didn't accomplish the task at all. While I'm disappointed that I didn't get to the task today, I see that I didn't shut it completely out of awareness, which to me is a positive sign. Ah, ever the optimist!"

Using the incantations and the ten-second centering process will make you more mindful, more centered, and more ready to proceed with the tasks at hand. Even if you don't get to a particular task today, you will have a much better shot at getting to it tomorrow if you make regular use of the incantations.

JENNIFER

"I chose as my difficult task confronting a recalcitrant daughter about completing her online traffic school test, which is due at traffic court in three days. This task has been especially hard because our relationship is strained and I needed to keep the focus on getting this task done without provoking an argument or

further procrastination. If she doesn't complete traffic school, the car insurance rates, which I am still responsible for, will dramatically increase. Many hard tasks came to mind, but this one was just the most immediate. I prepared myself, using Incantation 10 and also a few of the other incantations. But there was some delay, probably at least an hour, before the opportunity arose to speak with her. Still, all during that time, I felt calm and prepared. Actually, it turned out that she needed very little prompting. I had prepared the question: 'When will you start working on the traffic school course? It has to be mailed to court tomorrow.' It turned out that she had responded to an email I had sent two days earlier and had most of the test done. By coming to the interaction calm and prepared, I think it went especially well."

There is magic in being prepared, in feeling centered, and in experiencing yourself as equal to life's challenges. Use Incantation 10 to help you meet today's challenges.

Chapter fourteen

Incantation II: I Am Taking Action

When we feel uncentered we doubt our ability to make smart decisions or tackle important work. We may look busy, but our essential attitude is still one of passivity as we go through the motions and get dinner on the table or make our business calls. That passivity, in turn, causes more uncenteredness. We know that we should air a certain issue with our mate or make a certain career change but we feel too anxious and passive to proceed. Our inability to proceed causes us to feel guilty and more uncentered. This vicious cycle leads to depression, stress-related illness, and addictions. Eventually playing video games, shopping at the mall, or drinking at the bar start to substitute for real action.

Neither looking busy nor behaving compulsively is a real antidote to passivity. Taking real action is. When you aim yourself in an intentional way in the direction of an activity that holds meaning for you, whether that's having a chat with your child, volunteering at a homeless shelter, or getting your business off the ground, you sever the bonds that have been holding you down. Right action has remarkable curative power and is often the complete treatment for a bout of anxiety or depression.

If you find yourself sitting for too long on the sofa, get a right action in mind and use Incantation 11 to support your intention to act. Use it alone or in conjunction with Incantation 3, the name-your-work incantation. If you know that you should tackle a certain task but can't find the wherewithal to begin, use Incantation 11, with or without Incantation 10 as reinforcement. When you can't face that pile of bills, that leaky faucet, your coworker's complaints, or your creative work, and know that action and nothing but action is required, use Incantation 11.

Using Incantation 11

BARBARA

"There were two scenes in a novel-in-progress that I've been avoiding. I knew what I needed to accomplish in the scenes but because they hit pretty close to home on a personal level, I was afraid that writing them would prove too emotional an experience. I kept telling myself that this kind of emotional writing is

often the most powerful, and I told myself that I could have fun with them if I just approached them with the right attitude. But I still felt great resistance and the passivity you've been describing. I felt as if I'd have to move a ten-ton load to get to the computer and I just didn't feel equal to moving that load. I tried using various incantations and ended up just staring at the computer. I guess I couldn't trust my resources, frame it as a challenge, or whatever. Then I landed on Incantation 11. Just keeping in mind the idea of taking action finally seemed to help. It took some time to get going, but finally I did. I was able to get a draft of the first scene done. I don't know if Incantation 11 really did the trick, but I'm grateful anyway. I have that second scene to tackle and I'm not sure if it's going to be any easier this time, but I feel encouraged that if I keep my mind on taking action I'll be able to act."

You may feel like a ton of bricks. Maybe you don't believe that anything will get you moving, motivate you, or overcome your powerful inertia. You may be surprised, though. It isn't as if you actually weigh a ton! Maybe a few encouraging words will do the trick. Maybe a small, quiet, centering call to action is all that's needed. Give it a try.

ALICE

"My mother's been very sick recently. We needed to honor the way she wanted to deal with her illness but at the same time there were things we thought she ought to be doing that would afford her a greater chance of surviving. So we got very stuck not wanting to intrude but desperately wanting to pass along all the information and advice we were gathering. I used a number of the incantations to stay centered during this time, especially around trust and support, but that didn't help me tell my mother what I wanted to say to her. Then I tried Incantation 11, which sounded much gentler when I said it than when I see it written on the page. It allowed me to have a conversation with my mother that we really needed to have and that prompted her to take action that's probably been life-saving."

When you center and take action you cause wonderful ripple effects. You cause others to center and take action, too.

JODIE

"I really needed to uncover and straighten out my desk. I work at home and when the mess gets too great I'm in real trouble. But I couldn't make myself even decide that cleaning up my work space was a top priority. I have a difficult time making decisions, maybe because I was never allowed to make any as a child, so even something like deciding what to do next can present an obstacle to my

getting anything done. The pattern is this: My desk gradually fills up as I attend to my home business. In the meantime, the kitchen countertop gets filled up with unsorted mail, the dining room table gets overloaded with every manner of junk, and I begin to avoid those rooms and move to my bedroom, which soon looks as messy as my desk. Of course I can't clean the kitchen, the dining room, or the bedroom until the desk gets clean, but I'm stuck not being able to clean it and so nothing gets done. But I made up my mind to try Incantation 11. First I procrastinated and played innumerable computer games. Finally, after I had wasted a good hour and a half, I sat down and tried Incantation 11. I got up, walked into my study, approached my desk, veered off toward the computer, pulled myself back, and picked up the first item off my desk and decided what to do with it. Then I picked up the next item, and so on. I became increasingly more relaxed about the whole thing, until I reached the point where I wondered why I had been putting it off at all."

Maybe Incantation 11 won't "take" the first time. Maybe you'll continue procrastinating. The trick is to try and try again. After that half hour of television, give Incantation 11 another try. You may suddenly find yourself energized and called to act.

ADAM

"I needed to write a grant proposal. The first step was to design a rough-draft, one-sheet promotional flyer. The deadline was approaching and I wasn't sure if I was even going to apply. I thought about using the incantations to get myself started, but just thinking about using them brought up a ton of anxiety. I actually got up and left the room out of fear. But I stopped myself in the hall and, without having an idea that I'd choose that particular one, gave Incantation 11 a go. I went directly to my desk, panicked a little, used the 'resources' and 'trust' incantations to steady myself, and got started. I spent an hour working on it and got the rough draft done. What this proves to me is that my fear is just skin deep and that if I can just stop myself and turn to the incantations, I can tackle all the things that feel so scary. What a lesson!"

Maybe your fear is only skin deep. Wouldn't that be something? Maybe just a small call to action can dispel it instantly.

THERESA

"I was having this problem with my son, who's nine. I'd been through a divorce and my son and I had both gotten stressed out by having to move, by my new job with its longer hours, by him going to a new school, and by all the other painful things that came with the break-up. Then he started having trouble at school—

getting into fights. I knew I had to do something, but I didn't know what to do. The school suggested counseling, my mother suggested that I use the church, and my friends had all sorts of ideas. But I had the feeling that there was some action I could take, some simple action that would make a difference. So I used Incantation 11 to point me in the direction of the action I ought to be taking. I breathed-and-thought Incantation 11 a few times and then just headed for Bobby's room. I didn't know what I was going to do until I did it. What I did was hug him and hold him close. That led to us talking about the divorce for the first time, to both of us crying, and ultimately, to a change for the better in Bobby's behavior at school. I think that Incantation 11 not only helps a person take action but also points us in the direction of the action to try."

It could be that on a conscious level you don't know what to try. In that case use Incantation 11 to help you intuitively tap into your understanding of the situation.

MATT

"I'm a high school English teacher and I love what I do. But every Sunday night I find myself with a pile of essays to read and grade, essays that I've been carrying around all weekend. I don't know why grading papers feels like so much work, but it does. I ruin every weekend by not getting to those papers first thing Saturday morning

and polishing them off by noon. It only takes four hours to grade a set of papers but I must begrudge those four hours after working all week, or maybe the problem is something else entirely. I really don't know. But I made up my mind that I would try something new this past Saturday. Instead of packing up the papers and acting like I'd grade them at a café, I put the pile on my dining room table, poured myself a cup of coffee, and breathed-and-thought Incantation 11 about ten times. By eleven o'clock the pile was done and I went out and celebrated with a really big ice cream cone!"

If you change your routine in order to promote action, you may accomplish your goals without even needing to invoke Incantation 11. By setting himself up at his dining room table rather than popping those essays into his briefcase, Matt probably assured himself of a successful outcome. But adding Incantation 11 didn't hurt!

SAM

"I make the distinction in my own mind between being busy and being active. Busy is just doing what needs to get done, the boring things at work, the equally boring things around the house. I'm hardly ever centered doing those things and I get into lots of little accidents and dramas because I don't feel centered when I'm busy—even if it's just being prone to paper cuts! When I think of

myself as active I see myself riding my bicycle down a country lane, telling my daughters a fairy tale that I've made up—complete with different voices for the different characters—or hosting a party for friends whom I haven't seen in too long. There's joy for me in 'active' and meaning for me there, too. That's why Incantation 11 resonates so much for me. It's like a combination call to arms and an invitation to play."

Combine Incantation 9 (I am open) (to joy) with Incantation 11 (I am) (taking action) to turn your activities into pure joy.

Chapter Fifteen

incantation 12: I Return with strength

When you use the incantations to help yourself center, you instantly enter into a meditative state. One of the "tricks" of centering is to return from that meditative state not only centered and refreshed but also feeling powerful and equal to accomplishing whatever work comes next. Traditional meditation and centering techniques presume that you will return more centered, grounded, and present, but they rarely include an explicit transition step that returns you to the world ready to resume your work. Incantation 12's primary function is to help you do just that.

You don't return from your centering practice with nothing to do and nothing on your mind. You have everything before you that a serious, committed person who is living authentically needs to get done. You are becoming centered not to cease living but to live deeply. Living deeply entails engagement, activity, and work, all of which demand strength on your part. Therefore, after centering yourself with an incantation like "I trust my resources," you add on Incantation 12, "I return with strength," to quietly but powerfully propel you back into the world. What you are in fact saying is, "I trust my resources and now I return from my ten seconds of centering with strength."

It's not that you must then "do something significant" after you return with strength. You can sit quietly, nap, watch television, prune the roses, or do the dishes. You can do any form of "nothing" or "something" that you choose to do. You can just be, peacefully at one with the universe. At some point, though, you will have real work to do, work that makes use of your capabilities and connects to your goals, dreams, and desires. By regularly "returning with strength" you prepare yourself for that work.

"I return with strength" doesn't mean "Back to the rat race!" The intention of Incantation 12 is to build your muscles so that you feel equal to your real work. It can be used as a stand-alone incantation any time you want to make a clear transition from one activity or phase of the day to another. You can use it, for instance, after a business meeting when you want to get back to the work piled up on your desk, during the performance of a play you're in, or after lunch as you return to the office.

When you center you will feel stilled and also stronger. These are not contradictory ideas or mutually exclusive states. They go together beautifully. You want to move back into the world quieted, centered, and ready for the occasion. Practice Incantation 12 until you acquire a deep sense of its purpose. You may find it becoming one of your favorites.

Using Incantation 12

BETTY

"I've been using 'I return with strength' a lot and like it the best of all the incantations. Before suffering a career-ending back injury, I was a nationally competitive power lifter. Of all the sports I've engaged in over the years, that was the most challenging one. It used the most willpower and concentration, and it evoked the most fear and required me to focus substantial levels of physical and mental strength. Even though I can't lift heavy weights any longer, many of the lessons I learned in power lifting about skill, fear, pain, faith, persistence, and success stay with me. To say 'I return with strength' just feels so right. If I've felt tired, the 'strength' phrase infused me with faith in my ability to muster up energy. If I've felt out of sorts, it gave me the strength to meet my down mood head-on. If I've felt good, it feels like a return to vigor and effectiveness. I'm surprised that this whole thing makes so much sense to me and that I hadn't thought of doing anything like it before. Meditation never worked for me the way that this does."

Like Betty, you may be able encapsulate the lessons you've learned in life about discipline, persistence, and success in the phrase "I return with strength" and use it like a magic capsule to hold your secrets about mustering courage. How many times have you had to get off the mat after going down for the count? How many times have you surprised yourself by accomplishing feats you never dreamed were possible? Incantation 12 can hold all of those memories in one ten-second capsule.

ROB

"I used to practice Zen Buddhism and would even go on week-long sitting retreats. So Incantation 2, 'I expect nothing,' was congenial to me from the start. But nothing in Zen really prepares you for the sorts of real-world challenges I encounter as a hospital administrator. Zen is a quieting force, but stillness by itself doesn't equal power, which is why so many Westerners who practice Zen seem lethargic and even depressed. I love what Zen has to offer but it needs the added something that Incantation 12 provides. So I use Incantation 2 and Incantation 12 together for a twenty-second 'muscled Zen' experience."

Stillness is beautiful but it is not enough. If you mean to live according to your cherished principles you will have many challenges to face—challenges that require you to manifest your strength.

CAROL

"'I return with strength' means coming back to whatever I'm doing with a renewed ability to withstand the thrashing of daily life, to move closer to the eye of the hurricane instead of being caught in the chaotic outer winds. It means renewing my faith in myself and my ability to handle things. It also means not being tipped about by every opinion that falls out of someone else's mouth. I'm using Incantation 12 when I'm confronted by something important and when I'm feeling wishy-washy or easily affected by my surroundings. I like it that I have an incantation to use whenever I'm thrown off balance or when I'm feeling a little scared. Incantation 12 seems to tie up the free-floating loose ends in my life and anchors the whole centering process down."

You may experience a lot of free-floating anxiety in your life. One second the source of that anxiety might be a fleeting thought about an unpaid bill, the next second it might be the thought that you're running late. Fleeting thoughts of this sort keep us anxious all day long. When you notice one of these thoughts pop into your mind, immediately counteract it with Incantation 12. Return yourself to a state of physical and mental well-being.

BOB

"Yesterday it was difficult to find the strength to perform while dealing with a seriously sick cat who does not seem to be getting better. I went to the performance with much sadness and grief. I thought about what my job was and tried to strip it to its minimum. My basic job as a fool is to encourage smiles and laughter, which really means to give pleasure. So I named as my work 'I give pleasure.' I can do that, I thought. I have done it before, even when I'm sad. Then I added Incantation 12 to find the strength I really wasn't feeling. In fact, I did give pleasure and I found that I performed surprisingly well. I was even able to fill those moments between the gags and the tricks with some deep play, a sure sign to me that I was present and connected to my audience."

When you don't feel physically or emotionally equal to the moment, try Incantation 12. By announcing that you intend to return with strength, you marshal your strength and make the most of your depleted resources.

ELLEN

"To me 'I return with strength' means returning from a moment of centering feeling integrated, focused, and stronger for having made a conscious decision to do the work. It expresses an intention about how I'll do the work, about what elements are important to the process. This way of being is deliberate and implies that I'm thinking about things, not responding in an off-the-cuff way to some stimulus. As an orchestra musician who has to 'jump in' a hundred times during a performance, I pretty much automatically return with strength each time. The same isn't so true during rehearsals, when the conductor is demanding that we make changes. Then the mind has to come into it and not just muscle memory. It's during rehearsals that I find Incantation 12 particularly useful. Each time the conductor stops us and tells us what change he wants, I take a deep breath before we start up and feel my strength return."

Rather than responding to stimuli, you can wrest control of your thoughts, feelings, and responses by using Incantation 12. Something happens—the conductor cracks his baton like a whip and criticizes the string section—and rather than react to that something, you center yourself and decide how you want to be in the next moment: calm rather than agitated, strong rather than weak.

FAY

"'I return with strength' seems to say it all. For years I've said things like 'Time for work' and such phrases haven't helped me focus or center at all. For a while I used 'Life resumes,' but that had a rather sad tone to it, as if I'd left a higher state and now had to return to the mundane. A phrase like 'Strength and courage' somehow implied that whatever I was going to face next was going to be extraordinarily difficult, so it only made sense to use on certain special, particularly arduous occasions. I also tried 'authentic life,' but that was too abstract. 'I return with strength' does the work that all these phrases were intended to accomplish but didn't."

Maybe you've tried other centering phrases before without much success. Give the twelve incantations a try. Each phrase has been tested and proven resonant for a great many people. Some of them may work like a charm for you.

GRACE

"Transitions have always been hard for me, so using Incantation 12 seems a particularly important part of the centering process. When I race from one thing to another I don't acknowledge how hard transitions between work and home, my day job and my creative work, and being alone and relating with other people can be. Incantation 12 reminds me that I was somewhere internal

and now I'm returning to the external world, fortified and able to deal with reality in a clearer way."

Our days are a series of transitions, and each transition requires that we center anew and return with strength. Because we're obliged to handle so many transitions, Incantation 12 may prove your most useful centering mantra.

Chapter Sixteen

using the Twelve incantations

Whether or not you've tried out the twelve incantations and ten-second centering yet, you probably have a much better sense of how the process works having read the previous chapters. You've seen that people use the incantations as they see fit, using this incantation or that incantation according to personal preference and the nature of the circumstances in which they find themselves. There are no rules associated with using the incantations, no regimens, no multi-step programs, and no dogma. There is just the idea of employing a long, deep breath as a way to center and as a container for a specific thought. It's hard to present a simpler idea or one less encumbered by additional trappings. It's so simple that you may find yourself ready and willing to try out Ten Zen Seconds.

Each incantation embodies an idea about what leads to centering. If you can completely stop, you are on the way to centering. If you can trust your resources, you are on the way to centering. If you can consistently make meaning, you are on the way to centering. And so on. There is no pecking order and no need to rank the incantations. Each incantation is a stand-alone idea that, according to your mood and your situation, is the right one to try at that split second.

Choosing One Incantation

You might choose one incantation, memorize it, and use it for a period of time to see how the process works for you. Just read through the list of incantations (better yet, really practice all twelve of them) and then choose one as your personal centering incantation. A corollary idea is to create your own incantation and use it as your all-purpose centering mantra. We'll discuss this idea in detail in Chapter Eighteen. Clients and study subjects have opted for incantations like (right here) (right now) and (peace and) (light) instead of mine or in addition to mine and have found them invaluable. Before you create your own incantations, though, I think it would be wise if you tried out mine, as there is an important point to each one.

One place where you always create your own incantation is when you use Incantation 3, the name-your-work incantation. Here are a few uses to which clients have put Incantation 3:

LESLIE

"*To my surprise, I found myself naming (I release) (my family).
My son and daughter-in-law were visiting from Vermont, here for
my granddaughter's boarding school awards day and school vacation. My son told me that they wanted this time just with their
daughter, so that except for the awards ceremony I wouldn't be
seeing them. Intellectually, that made sense. Emotionally it was
tougher, even though I felt some lightness and relief at having time
to work. It felt right to use Incantation 3 to help me adjust to the
idea of not seeing my family as 'my work.'*"

RON

"*I had a hard day yesterday and then I had a bad night last night.
I tried some of the incantations to help me settle enough to sleep
but still sleep wouldn't come. So I tried Incantation 3 and used (I
am drifting) (into sleep) as my phrase. Funny to think about sleep
as 'work,' but I knew that was exactly the work facing me at 3:00
a.m.! Probably I would have fallen asleep anyway, but
Incantation 3 seemed to help a lot in the moment.*"

SANDY

"*I am beginning to see that I can name all kinds of work: cleaning out a kitchen cabinet, getting out my paints, drilling the holes
in a sculpture base, even taking a shower. There's something about*

the time sense that I really like. I'm used to identifying goals for an hour, a week, a month, even for my whole life, but this naming of the work is more present, more now. I like this process very much. Who would have imagined that thinking (I am taking) (a shower) could have such a calming, centering effect?"

Gaining Permission to Center

You can use one incantation on a regular basis. You can use several of the incantations, in one situation employing Incantation 1, in another Incantation 2, and so on. You can combine incantations, using two or three together. You can use a sequence of six incantations together that I call the Centering Sequence (described in Chapter Twenty-One). And you can create your own incantations. First, though, you need to nail down the basic idea. Consider the following hypothetical situation.

The pressure has been mounting on you at work, a task that was your responsibility got handled poorly, and you're feeling stressed out and even a little physically ill. Now your boss leaves you a voice mail message that he wants to meet with you in fifteen minutes. The message sounds a little on the ominous side. The worst thing about this sudden meeting is that you want to vent and you know that venting is the last thing you ought to do. There's nothing to be gained by complaining or trying to explain why the project went sour. You know that your better bet is to gather yourself and regroup before the meeting.

You decide to do a little ten-second centering. Which incantation should you use? Obviously "I am completely stopping" makes sense, as you've been rushing too much and know that really stopping is the only way to gather yourself. "I expect nothing" has its own logic, as trying to anticipate what your boss wants to talk about will only make you more anxious and defensive. If you could reduce your fear of a negative outcome by using Incantation 2, that would be a good thing.

You could center naming the meeting as your work, you could affirm that you trust your resources, you could assert that you feel supported, especially since your boss has always stood firmly in your corner. You could breathe-and-think "I embrace this moment" to remind yourself that there is nowhere to run and that it's in your best interest to be present. You could use "I am free of the past" to let go of the bad taste in your mouth that the failure of the last project has caused.

You might frame the meeting as a meaning-making opportunity, as a necessary and even useful step on your journey with this organization. You might try to turn the tables on the situation by looking not only for the silver lining but for the whole bar of silver by breathing-and-thinking "I am open to joy." Or you might announce that you feel equal to this challenge, whether or not you do, or affirm that you are about to take necessary action and that there is beauty in action.

You could get up, wash your face in the restroom, and invoke "I return with strength" to prepare yourself for the meeting. In short, you could use any of the twelve incantations. Each one has its logic, its purpose, and its special centering power. But what's vital is that you actually stop and center. *It matters much less which incantation you choose than that you choose one and use it.* What will really help is the act of using a long, deep breath for a specific thought, whether that thought is "I am completely stopping" or "I am perfectly fine." Marrying deep breathing with any resonant, affirmative thought will center you.

The main point is that you must obtain permission from yourself to stop and center. You might be thinking, "Well, why wouldn't I want to stop and center? Why would I fight that idea?" In fact you might fight the idea of centering for any number of important reasons. For one thing, being centered means being aware and we may really prefer pulling the wool over our eyes. Our defensive nature stands in the way of mindful centering.

You may not want to center because being centered is an undramatic state and you may prefer the devil-may-care dramas that staying uncentered permits. You can't recklessly drive your car in and out of traffic, throw the rent money away on lottery tickets, or fly from bed to bed or from needle to needle in search of excitement and also claim to want to center. Centering may be something you feel obliged to want rather than something you actually do want. Your real mantra may be, "I don't want to be centered, I want to be me!" In that case, you won't have permission from yourself to try Ten Zen Seconds.

When you're centered, you're equal to tackling your most important work. But maybe you fear failing at that important work. Maybe you're only paying lip service to wanting to write a novel or start a home business and fear that if you got centered you would have to risk making mistakes and messes. Thus, one lack of permission—the permission to fail—leads to another lack of permission, the permission to center. In such ways ten-second centering never gets its chance.

I'm sure you get the picture. We have many reasons not to want to center. We have at least as many reasons on the con side as on the pro side. You'll have to think through which way the scales tip in your case, a process that requires that you get under the radar of your defenses and engage in some honest self-analysis. I hope that you can do this. You might even want to name that as your work and use Incantation 3 to help.

Your goal is to gain permission to engage in the process. The technique is simplicity itself. A real desire to center is the harder commodity. Try out this new incantation for a bit: (I have permission) (to center). See what thoughts and feelings arise as you try it. In this way you may inaugurate a frank chat with yourself about the obstacles you put between yourself and the experience of centering.

Chapter Seventeen

choosing incantations

It's unlikely that you'll use all twelve incantations on a regular basis. What's more likely is that you'll land on two or three that become your centering charms. (You may also start using the sequence of six incantations called the Centering Sequence that I'll introduce in a bit.) Which two or three incantations should you choose to practice and learn? The answer, of course, is whichever ones make the greatest sense to you, resonate the most for you, and actually help you to center.

For instance, you might decide to employ Incantation 1 ("I am completely stopping") if you find yourself continually on the go, rarely make conscious transitions between one period of work and the next, and suspect that learning when, why, and how to stop are important growth areas. You might consider using Incantation 1 in the middle of a series of errands, before turning to your creative work, when you have an important decision to make, and when you feel your heart or your head racing.

You might decide to use Incantation 2 ("I expect nothing") if you habitually anticipate outcomes and get disappointed, if you try to control the behavior of others, if you work for praise rather than for intrinsic reasons, or if you're bothered by feelings of envy. You might think of employing Incantation 2 before an awards ceremony, a performance review, or a vacation; while waiting for opening night reviews or an important email; or before or during a first date.

You might decide to employ Incantation 3 ("I am doing my work") if you have difficulty moving from one project to another, procrastinate a lot, experience significant boredom or restlessness, or want to commit more energy and passion to your work. You might think of employing Incantation 3 before every business phone call, each time you enter your studio, when you want to achieve a desired state like calmness or high energy, or when you're confronted by an interpersonal challenge.

You might decide to use Incantation 4 ("I trust my resources") if you have difficulty believing yourself equal to the challenges that confront you; feel insufficiently talented, disciplined, or connected; are pessimistic about your basic nature or the basic nature of others; or frequently forget how many internal and external resources you possess. You might think of using Incantation 4 in situations that you usually find overwhelming, when taking a big risk, after a defeat, or any time that the idea of marshalling your inner and outer resources seems vital.

You might decide to employ Incantation 5 ("I feel supported") if you usually feel unsupported, if you've had to go it alone, if inviting others into your life is a challenge, or if you find it hard to acknowledge a helping hand. You might think of employing Incantation 5 before an interview or meeting, in work situations, when you collaborate or ask for help, and during financial, emotional, and physical crises that heighten your sense of vulnerability and isolation.

You might decide to use Incantation 6 ("I embrace this moment") if you live a scattered life; if you're aware that your mind is often back in the past, brooding about old mistakes or traumas, or already ahead of itself, worried about upcoming tasks; and if you want to feel more accepting of your circumstances. You might think of using Incantation 6 before giving a presentation or a performance, in the middle of a difficult conversation or interaction, upon entering a party or family gathering, or when you want to relax, meditate, or simply "be."

You might decide to employ Incantation 7 ("I am free of the past") if you feel burdened by unwanted memories, affected by past traumas, tied in knots by family intrigues and secrets, or want to put recent events to rest. You might think of employing Incantation 7 before family gatherings, when negative thoughts or traumatic memories intrude, when you find yourself in a situation that recalls an unfortunate experience, or when you feel on the verge of obsessing unproductively or behaving compulsively.

You might decide to use Incantation 8 ("I make my meaning") if you have an existential bent, find issues of meaning and value of paramount importance, want to strike out in a more meaningful direction, or like the idea of consciously investing meaning in the work you undertake. You might think of using Incantation 8 before stints of creative work, first thing each morning as a rallying cry, as a transition phrase to demarcate your day job from your evening's pursuits, or as part of the process of deciding to volunteer your time for a good cause.

You might decide to employ Incantation 9 ("I am open to joy") if your life feels joyless, if you want to consciously remind yourself to look for the joy in situations and experiences, if a low-grade depression seems to be dogging your heels, or if you seldom smile. You might think of employing Incantation 9 on the way to work, when you go out to a movie or a concert, on gloomy or rainy days, or whenever you want to invite joy into your life.

You might decide to use Incantation 10 ("I am equal to this challenge") if you're aware that you lack self-confidence, if you tend to retreat from risks, if you prefer playing second fiddle to taking on leadership roles, or if you have a dream that requires that you step out of your comfort zone. You might think of using Incantation 10 before tests and contests, before embarking on a hard task, as encouragement to have a serious conversation with a loved one, or during first dates and other firsts.

You might decide to employ Incantation 11 ("I am taking action") if you fear that you have a passive nature, if you procrastinate and put off your dreams, if you have trouble cracking through inertia, or if you've been feeling low and suspect that taking action will improve your mood. You might think of employing Incantation 11 after watching television, as you glance at the pile of bills on the hall table, when the thought strikes you that you'd like to support a cause, or when you recollect how long you've been putting off making a troubling phone call.

You might decide to use Incantation 12 ("I return with strength") if you're troubled by feelings of weakness and powerlessness, if you've been physically or emotionally unwell and want to encourage your recovery, or if fatigue or boredom are issues for you. You might think of using Incantation 12 each time you return to your desk or studio, after running errands as you pile out of the car with bundles, or when you come home from a business trip or a vacation.

As a useful exercise, read through the incantations again one by one. Consider which personality features each incantation addresses and whether those personality features constitute edges for you. If they do, that incantation may prove one of your mainstays. Next, think through what situations cry out for the use of that incantation. Do you face many of those situations? If you do, that's a good reason to choose that incantation as one of your favored few.

Here's how some clients came to choose their favorite incantations.

MAX

"*After looking the incantations over I intuitively knew which one I needed to focus on—'I trust my resources.' The first time it came up to use it I was in a sad, distressed mood. It was my birthday and we had our sick pet put to sleep. I was full of grief but I had a gig to perform. The first hour (it was a strolling gig where I entertained small groups and individuals while walking around) was pretty pathetic. I was not enjoying myself and consequently wasn't able to give joy to others. Suddenly it struck me to use the incantation. I took a break and breathed-and-thought 'I trust my resources' several times. This got me going again with more confidence. I had my skills, my props, my training, my audience, and the memory of a playful, loving pet. Later that evening I had the sense that I was weak and I knew to repeat 'I return with strength' a few times with long, deep breaths. That put me right back on course. I was able to entertain the audience, pay attention to chances for improvisation, and make creative choices. I even had fun. I think those two incantations are going to be my 'basic two.'*"

JOANNE

"*I chose 'I embrace this moment' as my number-one incantation. I chose it because one of my biggest problems is that I tend to lose focus on what's immediately in front of me. Instead my mind jumps to things I should be doing, things that I did yesterday, or things that I need to get around to tomorrow. Embracing the moment is really my biggest challenge and I've consciously decided to make it my number one priority by using Incantation 6 as my everyday incantation."*

LARRY

I was immediately drawn to 'I am open to joy.' My veterinary practice is so busy that I rarely take even a second to enjoy the animals I'm seeing, even though I love working with them. My day feels like a series of tasks punctuated by crises, with one animal in front of me and two more waiting in the other exam rooms, all day long, six days a week. I thought that 'completely stopping' was what I needed to practice, but that wasn't it. It was much more about noticing how much I enjoy what I'm doing. It's a crazy life when we don't experience joy when we're enjoying ourselves, but that's how it's been. So now I use Incantation 9 all the time, not closing my eyes but taking the full ten seconds to remind myself that I want to be open to the joy that caring for animals brings me."

You may have already intuitively decided which of the incantations are most resonant for you. If you have, start using them. See if your intuition is correct. If you haven't made any decisions yet, this is a good moment to decide. Read through the incantations again and choose one or two to practice. Then begin using them in real-life situations.

combining, customizing, and creating incantations

An excellent way to use the incantations is to pair them up for particular situations. The incantations stand alone but also work beautifully together. As an exercise, try to breathe-and-think any two of the incantations one after the other. What does it feel like to follow "I am completely stopping" with "I make my meaning"? To follow "I am doing my work" with "I expect nothing"? To follow "I am free of the past" with "I embrace this moment"? Play with the incantations in tandem and you'll land on some startlingly useful combinations.

When you want to make a transition from one stint of work to another, you might completely stop (Incantation 1) and then name your new work (Incantation 3). When you've mustered the courage to tackle a hard task, you might name that task (Incantation 3) and then remind yourself that you're equal to the task by adding Incantation 4 ("I trust my resources") or Incantation 10 ("I am equal to this challenge").

A sophisticated use of the incantations is to combine Incantation 9 ("I am open to joy") with Incantation 8 ("I make my meaning") to create a powerful existential antidepressant. By using these two incantations in tandem you announce that you have meaning to make, which helps rid you of the passivity that breeds depression, and joy to experience, which helps rid you of pessimism and negativity. If you prefer, you might use Incantation 11 ("I am taking action") instead of Incantation 8 ("I make my meaning"), in case the idea of meaning-making doesn't register for you.

One client liked to use the combination of Incantation 7 ("I am free of the past") and Incantation 5 ("I feel supported") before interactions with her parents. The latter helped remind her that she had a loving, supportive spouse and that she would be returning to him as soon as the ordeal of visiting her parents ended. Another client liked to pair the work-naming incantation with Incantation 11, "I am taking action." Just naming as his work the symphony he was composing didn't feel sufficient. He preferred to name it and then add Incantation 11 for emphasis.

One study subject built a small sequence out of three incantations, using Incantations 1, 3, and 12 together as the way to make the transition from her day job to painting in her studio each evening. First she told herself to completely stop, then she named her current painting as her work, then she "returned with strength" from pausing to center. A client, a well-known actor, found that he loved using four incantations together, employing "I trust my resources," "I embrace this moment," "I am open to joy," and "I am equal to this challenge" as his centering regimen before performing.

RALPH

"I've always been bothered by the idea that other musicians are better than I am. I don't believe that so much when I hear them play live. But like all musicians I have the memories of CDs in my head and CDs can sound so perfect, because they've been manipulated in the studio. No human practicing his guitar at home can ever sound that good. So when I practice, that's when I get these thoughts that other musicians are so much better. Unconsciously I'm playing those perfect CDs in my head and comparing my performance to theirs. Because at a conscious level I know exactly what's going on, I thought that I might be able to stop these negative thoughts by beginning each rehearsal session with 'I am rehearsing for an hour' and 'I expect nothing.' Just naming the work wasn't enough, because that didn't address the insidious comparison problem. But tacking on 'I expect nothing' was miraculous. That incantation silenced the CDs in my head and allowed me to practice calmly."

Another significant advantage of using two or more incantations in tandem is that you slow down for a longer period than if you used just one. You center for twenty seconds or for thirty seconds instead of for ten. You can gain this same advantage by repeating one incantation two or three times, a habit you may want to practice. Whether you opt to use incantations in tandem or to repeat one incantation several times, you'll benefit significantly from taking that longer pause.

Customizing Incantations

If you find that some of my phrases are close to resonant but not quite what you need them to be, customize them. Clients and study subjects have transformed Incantation 12, "I return with strength," into all of the following: "I am ready," "Time for work," "I am back," "I feel energized," and "Strength and courage." Folks who have had trouble with Incantation 2, "I expect nothing," have produced the following alternatives: "I demand nothing," "The outcome doesn't matter," "Anything is possible," "I am not invested," and "Excellent no matter what!"

You can hear how idiosyncratic these customizations are and how different one is from the next. Some are very abstract, some add ideas to mine (e.g., adding courage to strength), some are more affirmative (e.g., "Excellent no matter what!"), and some are uncongenial to my ear (e.g., "Time for work"). As an exercise, read through the list of incantations and put a check mark next to those that seem fine as they are. For the remaining ones, spend a little time customizing them until they fit the bill.

LESLIE

"I wanted to use 'I make my meaning' because I very much liked the idea of meaning-making, of taking charge of what I intended to value and hold dear. But the actual phrase wasn't working that well for me. It sounded like there was no meaning except the meaning that I make, which is maybe what you have in mind but feels problematic to me. So I played with 'passion' and 'value' as rough synonyms for 'meaning' and began trying out lots of phrases. I tried 'I make my passion' and 'I make my value,' both of which captured what I was intending but sounded too awkward. I tried 'I am a passionate person' and 'I value this moment' but those phrases felt like they were slipping away from the central idea. Then I landed on 'I choose this to value.' That was it! I would name my work using Incantation 3 and then follow that thought with my new Incantation 8, 'I choose this to value.' It had a regal feel to it and sounded just right!"

ADAM

"I'd been in a bad fire and was suffering from Post-Traumatic Stress Disorder, reliving that fire in nightmares and even sometimes during the day. So I knew that I wanted to use 'I am free of the past' as one of my mantras. But that phrase seemed to be about something else, more like if you had been abused or molested as a child and wanted to erase your childhood from memory. I wanted

freedom from a more specific thing. It occurred to me to try 'I am free of the fire.' But I didn't know if that might have exactly the opposite effect and bring the fire to mind all the time. In fact, that's pretty much what it did. I didn't like that feeling at all. So I didn't know which way to turn. Then one day as we were doing some routine maintenance the phrase 'I am healed from the fire' popped into my head. It was an immediately soothing thought, comforting on a deep level. I now use my version of Incantation 7 several times a day, and always first thing each morning."

Creating Incantations

Even though you may like my incantations exactly as they are, you may still want to create incantations of your own to supplement or replace mine. Creating your own incantations is an excellent practice and may prove more than mere exercise, as you may land on a phrase or phrases that serve you beautifully. Once you get in the spirit of Ten Zen Seconds and begin to appreciate the power of filling a long, deep breath with a meaningful phrase, you're likely to experience a strong urge to try creating incantations of your own.

LESLIE

"I guess it's my nature, but I decided to create my own incantations rather than use yours. I decided on 'I let go into this moment,' which has already proven very helpful. 'Right here,

*right now' is another one, and it's been equally useful in situa-
tions that have come up, for instance whenever I want to remind
myself that I need to show up with strength. Part of my job is
interviewing guests, and I've discovered that the interviews are
ten times richer if I center myself first with 'Right here, right now'
just before the guest comes on the air. Another incantation I've
created that's sort of long and cumbersome but that I like a lot is
'I am stopping right here and right now.' I think that its very
length forces me to take a really long breath, which is a good
thing for me. With the shorter incantations I can fudge some and
not really breathe, but not with an incantation this long! But 'I
let go into this moment' is my favorite, because 'letting go' of
things is extremely challenging for me, yet I know how important
surrender and detachment are for my mental and physical health.
So that's become my number-one incantation."*

Some people like to create one basic, all-purpose centering incantation of the following sort:

(I am) (centered)

(Grounded) (and centered)

(I go) (to my center)

(From) (the center)

(I am calm) (and centered)

(Perfectly) (centered)

(Centered) (and still)

SOPHIA

"I decided on the phrase (I am) (centered) and I'm loving it. Because the weekend has been full of special events and was somewhat tiring and because I nevertheless had work to do on Sunday night, I had to find a way to feel equal to tackling that work. I repeated 'I am centered' several times. My energy increased on the spot and I felt motivated to complete my tasks. The idea of having a simple system for inspiring myself to do something is exciting. I'll continue testing how well this particular incantation works for me, but considering how well it's worked already, I'm sure I'll be using it all the time."

Chapter Nineteen

BOOKENDS

A great way to use the incantations is to employ a pair of incantations to "bookend" a period of time and a stint of work. Use Incantations 1 and 3, the "stopping" and "working" incantations, at the beginning of the time period to lead yourself into the work. At the end of the work stint, use Incantation 3 in a new way—retrospectively—to celebrate having worked, and follow with Incantation 12 to return with strength to your everyday routine.

The time frame involved can be brief; for instance, a ten-minute break at work during which you intend to focus on a particular task or achieve a particular state. The time frame can be more like an hour, say the amount of time a meeting lasts, or even more like three or four hours, the amount of time you intend to spend writing an essay or training new employees. You use Incantation 3 to name the work you intend to tackle and also hold the additional thought that you are centering for a particular amount of time. This might sound like the following:

(I am writing) (for three hours)

(I will be calm) (during this break)

(I will speak my mind) (during this meeting)

(Two hours) (in the studio)

(At my desk) (for a good hour)

The added wrinkle of incorporating a time frame in the "name your work" step isn't a big change. However, using Incantation 3 a second time, at the end of the designated period as closure, does constitute something new. It's the first time that an incantation has a "backward look" or retrospective feel to it. To celebrate the fact that you consciously designated a period of time for a certain purpose, you include a "past tense" thought in the "name your work" incantation, for example:

(I worked) (well)

(I was present) (at that meeting)

(I consciously) (stayed calm)

(I bravely) (painted)

(Three hours) (of commitment)

(What fun) (that was!)

(I respect) (my effort)

This amounts to a new sense of centering. Because we rarely appreciate the effort we make or the work we do, we find ourselves rushing off to the next thing because "we haven't done enough yet." Using the incantations as bookends to frame and celebrate a period of time helps remind us that *we did just do something*. This is a centering thought that can lead to a deep sense of calm and that makes further running feel unnecessary.

Using the Bookend Process

KATIE

"I'm intrigued by the idea of stopping completely to acknowledge that I have completed something or accomplished something. Actually, this has been a new part of my experience lately. Usually I have my lists of what needs to be done, which breed more new lists, regardless of what gets checked off. But lately I have been listing whole projects separately, and as they are completed I cross them off and reflect a bit on the fact that I do accomplish a lot on a daily and weekly basis. After reflecting on the idea of bookending today, I'm thinking that there are additional things that I do regularly that I need to stop and acknowledge. Writing, meditating, having conversations about hard-to-broach subjects, maintaining friendships, caring for my aging mother, or taking action on creative ideas often do not make the usual projects list, even the

new list I've begun. I will make this practice of 'bookending' activities part of my process and watch to see how that changes my sense of self and my sense of accomplishment."

Try a book-ending experiment today. Use the incantations as described to frame a particular period in a special way. Give it some thought and set up your little experiment.

LORI

"Wow. Such a simple idea and I'd never considered it before. And, truly, it fits neatly with something I'd been turning over in my mind this past week—that I don't remember the good things that happen within a day. I'm so busy going to the next thing and dealing with the world of stuff I still have to do that I don't feel the successes, I don't feel like I make progress or that I'm doing well at all. To counteract this, I had just redesigned my daily planner to include a 'Joy Log.' At our writers group, our guest speaker talked about 'Marking the Moment' by reminding yourself of a success or telling someone else about a success, for instance by sending an email to a writer friend. So, the bookends approach really functions much like my Joy Log or Marking the Moment. You get a lovely sense of completion and peace and pride. I used this bookends approach to help me focus on a huge project redesigning an online writing group that I moderate. It's

a whole lot of work, lots of administrative pieces need to be developed, FAQs, and so on, and it will take many hours to accomplish. So I chose a couple of tasks and marked the beginning and the end. The cool thing was that I was going to quit (I had run out of time), but because I was going to mark the work done, I realized that if I did just a few more minutes of work, I'd have completed something that other people could review. It would make for a real stopping place and a real accomplishment. So I did exactly that and got some extra important work done."

Use the bookends approach to create real beginnings, real stopping places, and a real sense of accomplishment. This is a centering gift on many levels: you reduce your need to procrastinate, you work more deeply on projects, and you experience completely stopping after each work stint.

MIRANDA

"The first time I started to use the bookends approach, I intended to do the incantations as you instructed, but I got too excited to get started writing so I didn't take the time to do the meditation. I just set the timer for one hour and began to write. It amazed me that I stopped about a minute before the alarm went off. I realized that I had reached my objective without using the incantations at all, yet they were there in the background making it all possible. I definitely gave

myself credit and felt quite pleased that I had accomplished what I set out to do. The next time I wanted to try the bookends sequence, I made a point of following the instructions more carefully. I wanted to read a book that was helping me focus on structuring my work, to which I assigned a half-hour time limit. I used the incantations, naming as my intention that I would read the book for thirty minutes, and immediately after completing Incantation 3, opened the book. I worked for about forty minutes, completed the task, and used the incantations for closure, just as you recommended. I gave myself even more credit this time. I'm amazed at the way I can accomplish things when I use the incantations, with or without setting a time limit. I also like having validation for getting things done, even if I only get them partly done. I should also add that I was able to use the incantations while my husband was in the room reading. Three objectives achieved in one stroke: centering in front of someone else, working with him in the same room, and successfully bookending."

The bookending approach helps you work when you otherwise might be too distracted—for instance, in a public place—or while people are doing other things around you.

NIKKI

"I rarely stop to acknowledge that I've accomplished something. I'm certainly capable of berating myself for what I haven't done,

however. When I was still teaching, I used to keep a 'To Do' list on my computer at work. Every day I managed to scratch off a few items, but I usually added at least five each day. Thus, the list grew and grew. Soon it filled two single-spaced pages. I had categorized the items to better see what project I was working on at the moment, and I thought that the list was helping me to be organized. I now think that I was simply demoralizing myself. Lists are useful but I think that I didn't really know how to use the concept of list-making. I'm not sure I do now either, but these days I make up a daily list of two or three items and try to remember to pat myself on the back every time I accomplish something. My well-meaning parents seemed to focus on my negatives in their efforts to push me to do even more and I guess that old habits die hard. I really enjoyed trying out the bookends idea. I had dropped out of an online writing group in order to work on an article. The moderator of the group was kind enough to ask if I wanted to be removed from the group. I said no; and today I decided to use the bookends approach to get back in touch with the group. I used the incantations directly before signing on to the list to keep me from wandering elsewhere on the Net. I read a short story that had just been submitted that I know I'll enjoy critiquing. I used Incantations 3 and 12 afterward, and it gave me the time I needed to tell myself, 'You did it! You're not going to give up that group!' Ordinarily I finish one thing and race off to the next, but this time was different."

Even as you're breathing-and-thinking 'I return with strength,' you're likely to be congratulating yourself on having worked, remarking to yourself on how easy it was to get the task done, and fortifying yourself for your next important task. Ten seconds is a wonderfully expansive amount of time in which to think not only one good thought but several more 'in the background' as well.

PAULA

"Bookending is another example of how centering is so respectful of yourself and why I'm enjoying this process so much. I only recently began to stop and acknowledge accomplishments in my work routine, probably as a way to fight the sense of never-ending overwhelm that accompanies my job. Multitasking, while often necessary, does not provide a sense of reward or awareness, because you are always 'in the middle' of something and never notice when one thing stops and the next one starts. I have found that just consciously saying 'well done' makes a huge difference. Now formalizing or ceremonializing it through bookending adds a deeper sense to it. This is so great, learning to appreciate instead of rushing on."

You will only appreciate your accomplishments if you find the way to acknowledge them. Bookending is perfect in that regard.

Chapter Twenty

ten zen seconds centering exercises

In order to reap the benefits of ten-second centering you need to use it and, better still, acquire it as a habit. The exercises in this chapter will help you do just that. Choose one or two exercises, or as many as you like, and give them a try. The more exercises you try and the more often you give them a go, the more quickly you'll acquire the habit of rapid centering.

Overlearning One Incantation

One of the best methods to learn a new skill is to overlearn it, that is, to practice it even more than feels necessary. The old-fashioned way to overlearn an idea (yes, it was punishment, too) was to write on the blackboard a hundred times. In this way you really learned "I will not pull Nancy's hair" or "I will not throw chalk at the teacher."

This is still an excellent way to overlearn an idea. Choose an incantation that you think may work well as your everyday center-ing charm or pick one of the phrases you've created yourself and mindfully write it out a hundred times on a sheet of paper. Each time you write it, really hear it, feel it, experience it, and see your-self using it in a particular situation. Proceed through this exercise as slowly as you can.

An analogous overlearning exercise is to use your everyday incan-tation as many times as you can, even when you don't feel particu-larly uncentered. Choose a day and make a pledge with yourself that you'll center two or three times an hour, even if that feels weird, unnecessary, and even silly. If you do this, you'll see how little time ten-second centering takes and how good it feels to regularly center.

Memorizing the Twelve Incantations

Although children have to memorize for tests, adults do very little memorizing. Therefore, you may not feel very motivated to memorize the twelve incantations and you may even balk at the thought, as it may bring back unpleasant memories of studying for biology tests (the hip bone is connected to the . . .) and French tests (je suis, tu es, il est, elle est). Still, memorizing is key to the process, as committing the incantations to memory is exactly what you need to do if they are to be available when you want them.

You can just read the incantations over and over again until you have them memorized. Better yet is repeating them out loud. Even better is saying them out loud as you write them down, speaking and writing each one as many times as you feel able. This sounds like work and it is work, but the ultimate goal is so important that you may deem it time and effort well spent.

Try any method for memorizing that you like. You might turn the incantations into a jingle or set them to music and hum them or sing them until you own them. You might put them up on sheets of paper all around the house and commit to reading the list each time one of the sheets catches your eye. You might tape-record them in your own voice and set up times during the day for playing yourself the tape. You'll know that you have them memorized when you can remember them easily.

Teaching Ten-Second Centering

One of the best ways to learn something is to try to teach it. When we have to put an idea that we've been exploring into our own words and communicate it to someone else, we discover just how difficult teaching is and just how poorly we understand the ideas we think we know perfectly well. A physicist friend of mine summed up the difficulties inherent in teaching as follows: "I thought I knew thermodynamics until I had to teach it. Then I had to spend three hours every day preparing just to stay ahead of my students!"

Take it upon yourself to teach one other person the principles of Ten Zen Seconds. See if you can do that teaching without notes of any sort, which of course means that, at a minimum, you will need to have the incantations memorized. You may suppose that you'll be able to describe something as simple as the ten-second centering process without any hesitation and even without any preparation. But it may surprise you to discover that, when you try to explain it, you're not as clear or fluent as you expected you'd be. This discovery may prompt you to revisit the material and learn it more deeply.

What we usually do when we want to share an idea we've encountered in a book is to point our friends to the book. In addition to pointing a friend in the direction of this book, teach that person the ten-second centering process yourself. Demonstrate it as you go, showing him or her what ten seconds looks like, explaining what pausing for ten seconds to breathe-and-think feels like, and so on. If you do, you'll deepen your understanding of the process—and really help your friend.

Keep a Ten-Second Centering Journal

Teach yourself about ten-second centering by keeping a journal devoted to your experiences. You might set up the journal as a simple diary in which you write down your thoughts and feelings about being uncentered and about using the incantations to center. You might note which incantations worked the best, when they worked, when they didn't work, and, if you can tell, why they worked.

You might also go a step further. You might try to identify patterns of behavior that uncenter you: recurring uncentering situations that need special attention; daily, weekly, and monthly rhythms in your life that affect how well you center; and other relevant issues of personality and circumstance. This extra effort at self-awareness will pay great dividends and amounts to a mindfulness practice that in and of itself will help you center.

Another way to use your journal is to articulate goals for yourself and process how well you met your goals. You might set aside a page for each day and set some daily centering goals, for instance that you will consciously center before each of your business meetings or consciously demarcate lunch from the rest of the day by bookending lunch. Creating simple plans and setting straightforward goals are excellent ways to incorporate ten-second centering into your daily life.

Rehearse Upcoming Situations

Rehearsing upcoming situations in your mind's eye is an excellent way to prepare yourself for interviews, auditions, meetings, conversations, and other events that potentially provoke anxiety. If you become adept at mental rehearsing you'll arrive much calmer and better prepared. If you include centering in your rehearsal practice, you'll add an additional calming element.

Picture an upcoming event in your mind's eye. Maybe it's a meeting with your boss. Picture yourself at your desk waiting to take the elevator up to his office. Picture yourself sitting there calmly, using your incantations to center. See yourself ascending in the elevator and continuing your centering practice. Next imagine the interaction itself and plan how you'll field the questions you think your boss may fire your way. Try out various answers to each question until you land on the ones that serve you the best. Finally, picture yourself leaving your boss's office after the successful meeting, "returning with strength" to your desk and your work.

Get in the habit of mentally rehearsing upcoming situations and picturing how you'll use Ten Zen Seconds to help with those situations. It takes only a minute or two to mentally rehearse, and those few minutes will pay real dividends. You'll approach the important events in your life with more confidence, and you'll be much more likely to use the incantations if you have rehearsed them in your mind's eye.

Quizzing Yourself

An enjoyable way to practice Ten Zen Seconds is to quiz yourself on hypothetical situations and predict which incantation will serve you best. In the following situations, for instance, which incantation would you use? What's your rationale for your choice?

- You're trapped in a stopped elevator.
- You learn that your eighteen-year-old son has just been in a minor car accident.

- You're writing a novel and discover that you don't know how it ends.
- Your boss asks you to fly to Denver but you promised your daughter that you'd attend her soccer game that Saturday.
- Your mother has been talking your ear off for an hour and you can't get off the phone.
- You're dying to quit your job but can't decide if quitting is the right thing to do.
- You need to schedule a dental appointment but have been putting it off.
- You've just answered eight emails and, while you answered them, twelve new emails have arrived.

Instead of watching a television show after dinner tonight, take this little quiz. Or devise a quiz of your own. You'll gain a lot of insight into the ten-second centering process if you do. And you'll have some fun!

Tackling Something Hard

An excellent way to practice Ten Zen Seconds, while at the same time getting some work done, is to select a hard project—something complicated, ambitious, creative, risky, or otherwise difficult—and commit to using the ten-second centering process to help accomplish your goal. The project can be one at work, one around the house, an interpersonal matter (like having a hard chat with your child or your mate), or something connected to a long-held dream. It can take minutes or days, be intellectual or physical—in short, it can be any project at all.

One way to select this project is to ask yourself, "What have I been putting off?" If you've been procrastinating on a project or task, even one as undramatic as making a phone call or straightening up your work area, that's a good project to choose. Get the project in mind, think through which incantation or incantations you'll use and how you'll use them (before you begin, at different stages during the project, as bookends, and so forth), and proceed to center and to work.

Centering with a Buddy

If we're supported and held accountable we do a better job of sticking to our commitments. Usually we have to provide that support and accountability ourselves, serving as our own best friend and taskmaster. As a creativity coach, I serve these twin functions for my paying clients. You can enlist your own non-charging coach by joining up with a friend and agreeing to offer her your support, guidance, and feedback in return for hers.

One of the easiest ways to do this is by email. You can take turns starting out the new day by emailing the other a short, sweet email of the following sort: "I am going to work on completely stopping today. What are you going to work on?" Or "I'm using 'I trust my resources' as my everyday incantation. Are you still using 'I am equal to this challenge'?" It matters less what you say or how your buddy responds than that the idea of centering gets on the table each morning.

You can communicate with your buddy a lot or a little. You can play it by ear or set up guidelines. You can take turns leading, with you taking charge one week and your buddy taking charge the next, or you can follow and lead according to circumstances. There are many models to choose from for your buddy system. Have a chat with your buddy and decide how you want to operate as centering partners, then leap in and begin the process of mutual support and guidance.

Try out some of these exercises. They'll deepen your experience and help you commit to the centering process. Pick one right now and give it a whirl.

introducing the centering sequence

There are limitless ways to combine the incantations. You can use a set of two or three in a row to make a twenty-second or thirty-second chain that becomes your personal centering charm. You can combine different ones according to your mood and your circumstances. You can use one of mine and one of yours together. But there is a way of combining incantations that I think you'll find particularly valuable. It's using Incantations 1, 2, 3, 4, 6, and 12, in that order, to produce a one-minute Centering Sequence. This Centering Sequence works wonders to center, calm, and motivate you.

These six incantations make up the Centering Sequence:
(I am completely) (stopping)
(I expect) (nothing)

(I am doing) (my work)

(I trust) (my resources)

(I embrace) (this moment)

(I return) (with strength)

As the contents of the name-your-work incantation change each time you use it, the Centering Sequence has a variable look as you name specific work. A typical sequence will look like the following:

(I am completely) (stopping)

(I expect) (nothing)

(I am making) (that phone call)

(I trust) (my resources)

(I embrace) (this moment)

(I return) (with strength)

         –or–

(I am completely) (stopping)

(I expect) (nothing)

(I am off) (to write)

(I trust) (my resources)

(I embrace) (this moment)

(I return) (with strength)

         –or–

(I am completely) (stopping)

(I expect) (nothing)

(I intend) (to stay calm)
(I trust) (my resources)
(I embrace) (this moment)
(I return) (with strength)

I'm sure that the logic of the sequence is clear to you. Stopping is always the first step in centering. Next, you let go of expectations. Then, having let go of expectations, you name your work. Having named your work, you remind yourself that you have the necessary resources to accomplish that work. Then you settle yourself deeply into the present moment. The sixth phrase transitions you from your calm, centered state back into the world, ready to work (or to be).

Because it involves six different thoughts, the Centering Sequence takes some practice to learn and to master. In the beginning you may need to perform it with your eyes open, in case you have to refresh your memory with a "cheat sheet." But eventually you will remember the six phrases without needing to look at a piece of paper and then you can use it as intended, with your eyes closed. (You can also use it with your eyes open; for instance, when you're in public and don't want to "look funny.")

If you like pneumonic devices, you can remember the Centering Sequence in the following way. The first letter of each of the following six phrases taken together spell CENTER:

Come to a complete stop
Empty yourself of expectations
Name your work
Trust your resources
Embrace the present moment
Return with strength

Making use of this device means learning two sets of phrases, so it may prove simpler to learn the incantations through practice until they become second nature to you.

In reality the Centering Sequence takes a little longer than a minute, because there is the necessary preliminary step of choosing what work you intend to name in Step 3 and, often, the additional preliminary step of taking a few warm-up deep breaths before launching into the sequence. Some people also like to repeat one or another of the steps for added emphasis, often choosing the first step (because they want to really stop) or the last step (because they need an extra moment before returning) to repeat. So your one-minute centering tool may actually take two minutes to perform. But I hope that you won't find two minutes too much time to devote to centering.

I'd like you to experience the Centering Sequence right now. Before you begin, you'll need to name some work to include in Step 3, so take a moment and ask yourself the question, "What would I like to think of as 'my work' for the sake of this exercise?" When you have an answer, you're ready to begin. Be prepared to feel motivated to do the work you named, so set aside some real time for this exercise. Practice the Centering Sequence right now, taking your time and paying attention to the quality and length of your breaths.

Using the Centering Sequence

MONICA

"I found that I liked the sequence, though for some reason I felt a little sheepish at first. Then I stopped being skeptical and threw myself into it. With the first step I thought, 'Yeah, right. When's the last time I stopped?' With the second step I felt humble, if that's the right word, and it was a good feeling. For Step 3 I named (I am becoming) (a confident author) because lately I've struggled with feelings of fear and worry. Despite the fact that I know logically that I've written and published four books, some emotional part of me still thinks it's a fluke. Naming my work that way in the context of the sequence brought a real feeling of relief."

Jot down your experience of trying the Centering Sequence. You'll learn the sequence more quickly if you spend a little time processing your reactions to using it.

NANCY

"I found the sequence to be a positive experience, reminiscent of the Biofeedback Therapy I used to engage in (and pay for) to help me relax and reduce stress. As I practiced the sequence it seemed to get progressively easier to keep out distracting thoughts. The first step reminded me how pleasant stopping can feel in a life crammed with too much to do. The second step seemed really appropriate for a chronic perfectionist like me. It's delightful to do something for which you won't be judged and about which you don't have to judge yourself. For work I named 'going through last week's mail and papers.' It's a mundane activity and I don't usually do such tasks in the evening, but I've been putting it off. I knew I wouldn't get anything done tomorrow if my work area was still piled high with extraneous material. I felt mildly irritated having to name such mundane work and really wanted to name something more significant. Frankly, though, that kind of task is sometimes the most difficult to focus on—the chores you don't enjoy doing."

Tackling even the most mundane chore requires a certain measure of centering. Use the Centering Sequence to tackle cleaning out the bathroom medicine chest or the bedroom closet, tasks that aren't earth-shaking but that, if fretted about, produce stress.

OLGA

"At first I was trying to memorize the sequence, so I didn't stay very relaxed in the beginning. As I continued to practice, it became easier. I relaxed and was able to be clearer about the content. It must be that I think visually: I found that I was seeing stop signs, ivy-covered walls, brakes being applied, a horse being reined in, etc. as I began to slow down mentally. 'I expect nothing' brought with it a cosmic void, empty blue space, a desert. I didn't like these images, so Step 2 clearly needs some rethinking on my part. I like to say that I trust my resources and think I am self-sufficient but I don't really believe that. My inner resources become easily destroyed by outside influences. Years ago I wrote a lot of poetry. After a few years of immersing myself in those emotions, the words vanished. I want to be able to experience that immersion again and I think Step 4 will really help in that regard. I was also able to embrace the moment and it was a calm, peaceful experience. 'I return with strength' is a hope, a promise that I want to fulfill. I think I will use 'I am becoming a more dedicated artist' as the work I want to name. What I need is to take myself more seriously in areas where I want to change."

Using the Centering Sequence helps you live more authentically. You are announcing, "I mean to center and I mean to accomplish my work."

PAUL

"I'm really enjoying the sequence. My experience thus far has been completely positive. As I breathe deeply and think the six phrases, my body becomes relaxed and my focus in the present becomes stronger. The phrase 'I trust my resources' seems pivotal, because if we don't trust ourselves, then how can we trust the work (personally or professionally) that we are doing? So that phrase has the most resonance for me and I find myself repeating it two or three times, going to an even deeper place each time I say it. The work I named was (I am starting) (my business). I chose this because I have been wanting to start a certain home-based business for a couple of years and I just haven't begun, mainly because my day job is so hectic and consuming. The first few times I tried the sequence I 'merely' felt centered and peaceful. The next few times I felt energized, but I still balked at actually 'doing anything.' On the third day—and I felt really proud to be still practicing!—I went directly from the sequence to a new notebook I'd bought for the purpose and began to outline my business plan. That was the breakthrough. All my thoughts about the business came flooding out. I know that I am now really launched—and the Centering Sequence will accompany me on this journey."

Are you harboring a long-deferred dream? Use the Centering Sequence to revisit it.

ROBERTA

"Using the Centering Sequence went quite well, although it felt awkward at first. I know that the more I use it the more effective it will become. It also made more sense as I went along. Completely stopping was good for me—I really need that experience. 'Expecting nothing' suggested 'letting go,' which is a huge challenge for me. As to naming work, I chose (I am centered) (strong and whole). I've just been through an incredibly tough, painful year. I'm presently being treated for clinical depression and anxiety, which has lifted slightly, and that's a blessing, because I was told two days ago that I may have a potentially life-threatening illness. Naming my work this way is what I need to hear right now. I felt relieved and empowered that at long last I was acknowledging and addressing these deep needs. In the whirl and chaos of depression, you are in no position to 'address' very much constructively. The medication has begun to help, I think, as has support from others. I have a strong sense that the Centering Sequence will be extremely important to me also. Because of the very considerable challenges I'm now facing, this process engages me on many levels and I already consider it part of my 'survival gear.'"

The Centering Sequence can become more than just a centering tool. It can become part of your survival gear. Give it a try.

Chapter Twenty-Two

practicing the centering sequence

When an object is moving in a certain direction with a certain amount of momentum, it requires energy to change its course and even more energy to get it to stop. Conversely, when an object is inert, it takes considerable energy to get it moving. The same is true for human beings. This helps explain why something as deceptively simple as stopping for ten seconds to center—or, in the case of the Centering Sequence, stopping for a minute—can prove so daunting. If we have momentum—if we're rushing around—it takes real energy to get us to stop. If we're inert—a little blue, a little slumped in our chair—it takes a similar jolt of real energy to get us to move. How will we muster that energy?

The answer has to do with our ability to "hold an intention." Human beings can remember to do things if they are holding the intention to remember. How do we remember to pick up our daughter from school or to turn on the television at nine for our favorite show? Maybe a few people have a device that alerts them, but most of us "just remember" to do these things because we are holding them in a corner of awareness. We remember because we mean to remember. This "holding an intention" has a physiological basis and has to do with the way neurons get enlisted for various kinds of work.

Neurons "gather together" to accomplish work. Thought is a gathering of neurons. Memory is also a gathering of neurons. Intention is a special gathering of neurons. Neurons form smaller or larger "clouds" of neurons that coalesce and disperse according to what we are thinking, feeling, remembering, and intending. "Holding the intention" to do something is the exact equivalent of enlisting neurons to accomplish that task. A certain number of neurons are enlisted to remind us to pick up our daughter—if we hadn't enlisted them, we would "forget." When we hold the intention to use the Centering Sequence we energetically gather up neurons and enlist them for this specific purpose. Then, when they're needed, they provide us with the thought, "Okay, center now!"

Begin by memorizing the six phrases. Next, name your intention. Say, "I will use the Centering Sequence at least three times today," "I will use the Centering Sequence as soon as I get to work," or something similar. Underline your intention by saying, "I intend to use the Centering Sequence!" If you are willing to say that out loud, even better! At the end of the day, report to yourself on how well you held your intention.

Practicing the Centering Sequence

STEPHANIE

"I'm finding the Centering Sequence an excellent centering tool. Before using it, I was feeling very depressed. I was sitting on the floor crying and thinking a lot of negative thoughts. As soon as I started doing the sequence, I started to lose these thoughts. I kept doing it until those negative thoughts stopped creeping in and I'd memorized the sequence. I felt a tingling sensation in my hands and my arms and a physical sensation of peace in my heart. It's the same feeling that I have after doing an energetic treatment on someone. I felt like my energies were balanced. As I practiced the sequence I became more relaxed and started breathing more deeply. For a while I found myself thinking ahead to the next phrase or thinking other thoughts but I stopped doing that by the end of the session. I felt myself going deeper each time, as if I were entering a hypnotic state. I'm stronger and more resolved now than I was several minutes ago. I feel that I can control my feelings and moods and not let others bring me down. The affirmations are very powerful, especially the one about trusting your resources. I think that the sequence encourages you to believe in yourself and to stay focused."

The language of the incantations encourages you to believe in yourself. The more you use them, the more self-encouragement you'll experience.

TINA

"Trying the sequence today, at first I found that I was hurrying my breaths. I had to keep repeating the first phrase until I could feel myself actually slowing down. There was certainly a real resistance to stopping. I wanted to read my email, check my calendar, or look at my bills. I wanted to keep busy. Then, with Step 2, came relief. I liked knowing that there was nothing to expect. I had no goal, nothing to achieve. It felt like a burden being lifted from my shoulders. Step 3, naming my work, was tough. I named 'organizing my calendar' as my work, but that didn't feel right. Then on Step 4 I got confused. I wasn't sure what resources I was trusting. Embracing the moment was much better. I thought, I am doing exactly what I want to do in this moment. With the last step, I felt that the meditation was complete and that I was returning to my busy life with some emotional strength. All in all a mixed success— but a success nonetheless."

You may not flow right into the Centering Sequence, especially if stopping is a real challenge for you. In that case, work your way into it by taking as many preliminary breaths as you need. You can think a thought like "I am completely stopping" as you take these transition breaths or you can think nothing at all.

VIVIAN

"Today was one of those days when things were rolling along smoothly, so I was fairly relaxed and grounded when I did the sequence. The choice of words felt comfortable and on target. As I memorized the words I was able to feel them with more conviction. On Step 1 I felt myself being able to suspend interaction with the outside world. On Step 2 I felt permission to release expectations that add pressure and the possibility of disappointment. For work, I named 'A loose, creative painter.' I'm working to change my painting style from one that is tight, precise, and based in 'realism,' which had been drilled into me as the 'correct' way to paint, to one that is more edgy and free-flowing. I experienced a lot of happiness at the possibility that this may be a tool to help me be more experimental in my art."

The Centering Sequence is a perfect support to help you with big challenges and changes. Because it takes a full minute to use, you give yourself time to ready yourself for even the hardest work.

WANDA

"I immediately felt a kinship with the sequence, probably because of my meditation practice and the benefits I reap from that. It also reminded me of something I used to do several years ago, culled from some long-forgotten book, which involved thinking 'I inhale strength, I exhale fear' while breathing long and deep. But I really appreciate the 'sequence' part of the Centering Sequence. It's thoughtfully constructed to take me from the work-a-day world of eternal busyness and worry to a calm spot, and then bring me back again. Yesterday I was feeling bereft. I was sitting by the harbor, which was helping a bit, but then I suddenly remembered the sequence and closed my eyes and worked it a couple of times and felt better. It's another tool I can use to gain stability in an unstable world. When I don't have enough time for thirty minutes of formal meditation or can't be walking through nature, I can quickly achieve a place of depth and stillness by means of this handy sequence."

When you need it, you "suddenly" remember that you have the Centering Sequence available to you. This good luck is more likely if you commit to regular practice.

JASON

"While I was sitting on the subway today and struggling to keep a positive attitude as I headed to a meaningless, soul-sucking job, I remembered the Centering Sequence and gave it a whirl. Later in the day, as I raced from one boring task to another, I paused again to do it. And when I tried to make the transition from activities borne of necessity (day job) to activities needed by my soul (writing), I performed the sequence. Each step held meaning for me. I am completely stopping: I need to remember to stop in a physical sense, as I do race around a lot, but most importantly, to stop mentally, since my brain tends to spin off negative stories. I expect nothing: so important to think/feel this one. Expectations bring me much suffering, even when I think I have limited them. And the variable step—excellent! This makes the sequence adaptable to whatever the issue of the moment is. A couple of the phrases I've used are (I intuitively know) (the right path to take) and (I am) (a creative person). I trust my resources: here I'm reminded that I really do have resources, both internal and external, which will help me achieve whatever I've addressed in the previous step. And it's so necessary for me to believe not only that I have resources, but that I can trust them, since trust, or faith, or whatever you want to call it is very hard for me to maintain. I embrace this moment: my meditation practice has helped me with this a great deal but it's still something I struggle with constantly. It's crucial

for dealing with what's happening in the here and now instead of projecting and spinning out some future story or lamenting some past mistake. I cannot be reminded of this enough. Even when times are difficult, the actual reality of what's happening in the moment is much more manageable than the extreme scenarios I've created in my brain. And then, I return with strength, which is a beautiful way to make the transition back to the external world."

Each step of the Centering Sequence holds real meaning. If it happens that a step doesn't hold meaning for you, try eliminating it or replacing it with another phrase. Your sequence might be four or five phrases long; there is no magic number.

ABBY

"In addition to trying the Centering Sequence when I feel scattered or pulled in multiple directions, I've used it in a couple of other ways. One is as a wake-up device—a transition into the new day. I'm not by nature a morning person and I tend to be slow to transition from sleep into wakefulness. In fact, sometimes I think that getting out of bed is the hardest work I do all day. I've found the Centering Sequence a helpful motivator. I go through the process of breathing in and out the six steps, and this helps to convince my lazy brain that it really is daytime and that I really must do something about that obvious fact. For naming the work, I use a phrase like (I

am beginning) (a wonderful day) or (I arise with) (energy and enthusiasm). The other way I'm using the sequence is as a gearshift to move me from one project to the next. As a freelance writer, working mostly on organizational communications for clients, I often have several projects going at once. When I've delved deeply into one project, it usually takes me a lot of time to shift my attention to another. The Centering Sequence makes it easier to move back and forth between Project A and Project B. Excellent!"

Try using the Centering Sequence first thing each morning. Can you think of a better way to start your day?

---

customizing the centering sequence

The structure and phrasing of the Centering Sequence have been designed with care. It's nevertheless possible that you may want to tweak the phrases or replace some of the phrases with other ones. One of my phrases may grate on your ears, connote something negative, or otherwise detract from your centering experience. Or you may find that you like repeating certain phrases more than once or that by eliminating a phrase or two the sequence makes more sense to you. By all means personalize and customize the Centering Sequence until it fits like a glove.

Following are reports from clients and study subjects about their customization efforts. After you've read these reports, practice the centering sequence a few times and begin to think about what adjustments, if any, you want to make. It's not incumbent that you make any adjustments—the Centering Sequence may work splendidly for you exactly as it is. But if some changes are called for, by all means make them.

Customizing the Centering Sequence

SARAH

"I decided to tweak 'I trust my resources.' The word resources is used a lot in business as a substitute for assets. Often people are referred to as 'resources.' I think I probably have a negative connotation associated with the word resources based on my corporate work. Probably if I gave the phrase a chance I would have gotten over my distaste and maybe I'll go back to the original sequence, but for now I'm using 'I trust in abundance' instead of 'I trust my resources.'"

If a word in the Centering Sequence carries the wrong associations, substitute a word you prefer.

DIANE

"There is a sense of clarity and rhythm across the majority of the phrases, because most start with 'I [verb]' with the second half of the thought modifying the first in a way that breaks smoothly across an inhale and an exhale. The only one that didn't seem smooth is (I am completely) (stopping). I've changed (I am completely) (stopping) to (I stop) (completely). That sounds a little odd but I think it's an

improvement. At least I'm going to give it a whirl and see if a change made for the sake of consistency is actually a smart change to make."

Part of the process of using Ten Zen Seconds is finding the incantation language that works best for you. Be patient and consider that your first centering efforts are experiments. The journey that you make to find the right language will teach you a lot about what actually calms and centers you.

JEAN

"I began by having trouble with the line 'I am completely stopping.' Every time I thought those words I got this rush of fear because completely stopping to me signifies death. A pause is one thing, a total stop is another. I kept trying to tell myself that the line referred to a certain kind of pause, not a complete stop, but it just wasn't working. So I tried a phrase with 'pause' instead to see what would happen. What I discovered was that after I tried my own language I returned to your line and it felt fine. Now I am enjoying the sequence and find it very soothing. I think that what happened originally was that I was focusing on slowing my breathing and thinking about 'stopping completely.' The two linked together in my mind and resulted in those thoughts of death. By trying my own language and then returning to yours, the problem went away."

You have more than permission to create a Centering Sequence that works well for you. You have that responsibility.

MARTHA

"I really like the phrases and find them very quieting and calming. Only I'm thinking of using 'I demand nothing' instead of 'I expect nothing' because of the connotations the words have for me. To tell myself not to demand something means I need to stop useless or negative energy. If I stop demanding, then I actively let go and things occur of their own accord. 'Expect nothing' has a downside feel to it for me, kind of a whimper. I know that's not how it's meant and I can hear it the 'right' way, but I just like the concept of stopping the demand more."

It's not easy to get clarity on the difference between working hard to achieve goals and needing to achieve those goals. Find the language that makes this distinction clear to you. Your ability to center hinges on your ability to detach from outcomes.

JONATHAN

"The job of customizing the Centering Sequence is built right into it because you have to name a new work phrase each time you use it. That necessity makes the sequence fresh and new each time and makes the other phrases more acceptable. It's as if I can buy your phrases just

so long as I get one to tinker with. It's amazing the range of ideas that fit into the work phrase. I've used 'I am driving slowly,' because I can't afford to get another ticket. I've used 'I will mow the damned lawn,' a phrase that was centering because it allowed me to vent a little about how chores just keep piling up. And I've used 'My hobby is important,' because I had to convince myself that it wasn't selfish to spend a little time on my photography. So the Centering Sequence feels like 'mine' each time I use it because of the work-naming step."

Jonathan is right. The Centering Sequence has to be customized each time you use it, since the work-naming step is empty until you fill it up.

ADAM

"I find that it helps to repeat each step in the sequence until it's easy to breathe and my mind is empty for that step. The first time I say the phrase I don't really hear it or feel it but the second time I really do. So I've turned the six-step sequence into a twelve-step one. Obviously that makes it take a little longer, but the two minutes that I devote to centering feel well worth the investment. Also, repeating the phrases helps me remember the sequence. I know it perfectly well now, but the process of repetition is helping it sink in even deeper."

You might want to give Adam's version of the sequence a try. If nothing else, it will help commit the phrases to memory.

SANDRA

"Initially, I repeated the entire sequence but it left me feeling uncentered. I changed 'I trust my resources' to three different phrases: 'I trust my resources,' 'I trust myself,' and 'I trust my source.' That allowed me to focus on specific aspects of my resources. Now I like this step a lot and sometimes I even involuntarily smile with anticipated pleasure. I've also added 'I return with purpose' to the end, so I have two phrases that end my sequence. That makes my sequence nine phrases long and seems to suit me perfectly."

Your version of the Centering Sequence may be shorter or longer than mine. As long as it feels substantial and centers you, it's the right length.

JOY

"The 'trust your resources' step presented a big problem for me. Every time I went through the sequence, I absolutely hit a wall when I got to it. The word resources felt hard, metallic, and cold. It made me think of 'return on investment' and a term I really hate: 'human capital management.' So I tried 'I trust my own

wisdom,' which was better, 'I trust my inner voice,' which was good, and then 'I trust my inner knowing.' That phrase hit it exactly for me. It speaks volumes to me on many levels."

A phrase that "speaks volumes" is beautiful to own. Language rich in personal association deepens the centering experience.

ADAM

"I ditched the phrase 'I embrace this moment' and instead use 'Right here, right now.' I would think of embracing the moment and imagine the moment as something external and discrete, something that I could physically embrace. Because I'd rather not conceive of the moment as something outside myself but as something that exists within, I changed the phrase. 'I embrace this moment' was working well enough, but I guess I just like 'Right here, right now' better. I also use 'Right here, right now' as my basic incantation. It is doing a wonderful job of centering me."

A complete ten-second centering program includes using one or two incantations as your everyday centering charms, knowing all twelve incantations so that they are available to you, and employing the Centering Sequence as a more substantial centering device. See if you can put this complete program into place.

LITA

"I find that I like to repeat my line about my work at the end of the six breaths, making a total of seven. (I am working) (on my presentation) or (I am working) (on chapter four) are the lines I use most often these days. By the time I go through the entire sequence, I'm usually feeling peaceful and ready to go, but adding a little nugget about the work turns me from the Centering Sequence directly to the task. I think I'm supposed to be getting that from the line 'I return with strength,' but telling myself what exactly I'm returning to seems to give the sequence a little more zip."

Lita's addition is another excellent example of the customizing process. If more zip is needed, add that zip.

Chapter Twenty-four

centering in public

You may be finding it hard to practice the incantations and the Centering Sequence even in the privacy of your own home, because new habits are hard to inaugurate. But it may prove even more difficult to use Ten Zen Seconds in the world, where social anxiety, cultural injunctions, and "how we look" enter the picture. Few people are willing to stop in the middle of a busy sidewalk, blithely let foot traffic pass around them, and do something "in the mind" for a full-minute or even for ten seconds. In our culture, how conspicuous that would look!

If you feel too self-conscious to use ten-second centering in public, you'll likely have a lot of trouble getting centered in life. Ten-second centering is not something you make use of only at home as a practice and rehearsal tool. You want internal permission to use it whenever you require it. This sounds obvious and yet it needs to be emphasized. No centering strategy will be of much use to you if you can't use it when you actually need it.

Will you use the incantations in the car with the kids aboard? Will you use them before a business meeting, after a business meeting, and, most importantly, during a business meeting? Can you acquire permission from yourself to use Ten Zen Seconds no matter what's going on or who happens to be watching? It would be a good thing if you could. Your goal is not to be centered just for a few seconds early in the morning or after dinner. Your goal is to be centered all day long. To achieve this goal, you must gain permission from yourself to take the incantations public.

Maybe you'll look conspicuous and maybe no one will notice. Maybe you'll look a little ridiculous and maybe you won't earn a second glance. Either way, you need permission from yourself to center in public. This permission is itself centering. By eliminating the pull to look the way society wants you to look, a background social anxiety that so many people experience constantly, you rid yourself of a ton of "shoulds" and a significant portion of the anxiety coursing through your system. Suddenly you feel powerful in public—and relaxed.

The least difficult public use of Ten Zen Seconds is in a "public but private" setting, say when you're sitting alone on a park bench or writing in a café. Then your only worry is about how passing strangers or anonymous café denizens will view you. The most difficult use of Ten Zen Seconds is at work, when your worry is not just about how you look but about how your behavior might affect your business relationships and your livelihood. Somewhere in the middle is actively centering in the presence of family members or friends—though for some people this may prove the most difficult. Let's call these three situations:

1. Anonymously in public
2. With intimates
3. Doing business

Today I'd like you to try out ten-second centering in the easiest of these three situations, namely "anonymously in public." Although this is the easiest, it may not feel at all easy to expose yourself to a minute's worth of scrutiny as you sit at a café table or stand in a supermarket aisle engaging with the incantations. Still, I hope you'll make the effort. If you accomplish this centering feat, try centering tomorrow in a "riskier" setting; for instance, at work or at lunch with friends. Learn to center in the world, as that is where centering needs to happen.

Centering in Public

JUNE

"Taking the sequence public is a great step! Absolutely, you must trot the incantations out into the real world. This isn't about building an altar where you light candles and listen to flute music and the world can't reach you. This is your inner

altar. You take it with you. You use it to better interact with the world and be the person you want to be and live the life you want to live. I'm the founder/leader of a group of fiction writers and we meet in a library. Before the meeting, after tables and chairs were set up, I went out into the library, sat down, and did the Centering Sequence. Very easy. Then, midway through the meeting, while people were talking and I was functioning as facilitator, I did the sequence again. Since I had to pay attention to the meeting, I sort of split my attention between the sequence and what was going on. It reinforced my role and my sense of relaxation. I really wanted to stay present with the meeting and not be so busy leading, coordinating, moderating, etc. This often happens, as my energy is spent on these duties and I don't get to sit back and enjoy being with peers. By using the Centering Sequence I successfully stayed present and I felt renewed at the end of the meeting, not drained."

You can center even as things are going on around you. The more things are swirling, the more you need to center! Learn how to center "in the moment" no matter what a ruckus life is providing.

KAREN

"I had already begun using the incantations in public, for instance in church and at church vestry meetings. I've also found it marvelously useful in traffic jams and on the road when I would rather be somewhere else. Today I used them standing in line at the butcher shop and then again at the grocery. I didn't use it in the aisles, though, as they are too narrow and I would have blocked other customers on a busy Saturday morning! Oddly enough, I don't imagine that I look very different from anybody standing around looking harried. In other words, if I am doing a relaxation/centering technique, do you think all the other crazed people in line are looking at me? I don't think so. Using the Centering Sequence in public has been a good experience. Stopping and calming myself is something I should have been doing for years! Duh, why didn't I think of that?"

If using the incantations in public feels hard, try something simpler today. Just shut your eyes for three or four seconds in a public place. See if you can do that. When you open your eyes, see if anybody has noticed. What's your guess? I'll bet that everybody will be doing precisely what they were doing a few seconds ago.

LESLIE

"I had been using the Centering Sequence in public, while driving (yes, with my eyes open), in coffee shops, and at work in my office (which is mostly private). It's not particularly hard to do and I don't feel conspicuous doing it, as I spend a great deal of time doing things independently and in private. Nor do I always feel the need to stop and close my eyes to get centered. I have found that this practice has reminded me to notice when I am not feeling centered and to do something about it rather than to continue feeling scattered, anxious, or unfocused. I've had a couple of experiences lately with anxiety, the kind that knots my stomach up in an instant and doesn't seem to be caused by anything in particular. I've managed to use the incantations at these anxious times, which is kind of a marvel. For instance, I was about to make a phone call to Mexico from my office and I was feeling anxious about my Spanish, as well as anxious about talking to the friend I was calling. I decided to 'trust my resources' and 'feel equal to this challenge' and was able to calm and collect myself. The call went very well. I was able to easily understand my friend and express myself in Spanish and my overall nervousness while making the call was lower than it has ever been."

One of the blessings of practicing ten-second centering is that you'll notice much more quickly when you're feeling uncentered. Just noticing is a big deal, as then you're just a breath and a thought away from regaining your balance.

MIKE

"Today I tried ten-second centering at home while my wife was in the room. I thought that this might be the most public I would get today, and I also felt that I had already done the incantations in anonymous situations, so it was time to go to the next level. Later we went to the movies and I did it during the movie, because people were talking in front and distracting me from the movie and I was getting stressed. I didn't feel like that was enough public practice, so I did it standing outside the car at a busy gas station on our way home. In all these circumstances, even with my wife who sees me act ridiculous all the time, and even in the dark movie theater where nobody was watching me, I found it hard to concentrate. I was easily distracted. I was self-conscious. And I didn't really go deeply into the phrases. I just went through the motions without much awareness of the meaning of what I was saying. I only closed my eyes in front of my wife. I can see that this will take a lot of practice for me. I'm someone who has a great deal of background social anxiety. I even have problems doing an effective warm-up before a performance if there's a chance someone

might walk through the backstage area—even though I know I could injure myself or give a poor performance if I don't warm up. I see that social anxiety is a big issue in my life and something I really need to get a handle on."

If you find it hard to center in public, that difficulty is providing you with a wealth of information about your basic anxiety level. Take that information to heart and make a pledge with yourself to get a handle on your social anxiety.

NORA

"I've had a couple of medical appointments recently, so I used the Centering Sequence as I waited to be called in to see the physician. I also tried it at a group picnic yesterday. I've reached the point in my life where I'm not overly concerned with what people who don't know me think of me. I've been in the habit of standing on one leg while waiting in the supermarket line (to improve my circulation), and I've found that most people are so concerned with themselves and what they're doing that they don't pay any attention. Also, I live in a city, which makes my behavior even more anonymous. Yesterday I chose to use the sequence at the annual picnic of the Unitarian church I attend. That seemed like a more challenging setting than a medical waiting room, as I knew most of the people there, at least by name or sight. Unitarians are accepting of just

about anyone, so I knew that no one would be bothered even if he or she noticed that I was doing deep breathing. As I didn't have to say the phrases out loud, I simply waited for a moment when others were engaged in conversation. The centering helped me focus on the moment, on the beautiful day, and on the people with whom I enjoyed being."

You are in control of your centering practice. You can center now or, if you prefer, you can wait five minutes until people are no longer addressing you.

PAT

"A few days ago I was doing 70 mph in the carpool lane and one of those massive SUVs on steroids stayed right on my bumper. I was maintaining a few car lengths between myself and the car in front of me and I guess the driver behind me thought I should close the gap. I felt my anger rising because I had two children in the back seat and they were clearly visible. I was trapped until I could reach a spot where the lane dividers allowed me to move out of the way. Using the Centering Sequence really helped me regain my composure. I also used the sequence last week when I took my dad to the doctor. Dad is strong-willed, weighs two hundred pounds, and has a habit of running over my toes with his wheelchair when we sit in the waiting room. When I call his attention

to it he shrugs it off and tells me it's no big deal because I have another foot. The sequence helped me keep my cool. I'm beyond worrying about how something like this looks in public. I doubt that anyone pays attention."

Center wherever you find yourself, any place, any time.

RACHEL

"Yesterday I used the Centering Sequence on the way home from a disturbing movie because I was upset by some of the imagery but mostly because there was a potential problem brewing with my daughter who's returned home to live with us. I wasn't sure what we'd walk in on when we reached home. That had me full of dread. My husband didn't notice my eyes closed; or, if he did, he thought I was resting. Centering on the drive home helped me feel more capable of dealing with this difficult daughter. Today I used it in church before the service started, again because of this same daughter. There was a problem overnight, another piece of our ongoing conflict with her. In church, perhaps because of the setting and the work that I named, the most important part of the sequence turned out to be the 'trust' step. I needed to remind myself that somehow, some way, this kid of mine was going to be all right and that I was going to survive her living with us, how-ever long that might be. In the past two weeks I've used the

Centering Sequence to support me during the following: taking three cars in for servicing, successfully getting our health insurance reinstated after a six months' lapse due to a clerical error, one daughter's car accident, another daughter's acting out, about ten nights of insomnia, my mother's health taking a turn for the worse, and some scheduled invasive medical testing. None of it was easy and much of it will continue to cause me worry for months to come. But I've probably avoided at least 50 percent of the wear and tear on my physical and mental health by centering."

Make it your goal to practice the incantations in public every chance you get. Think of how much emotional wear and tear you'll save if you do!

centering and Healing

Ten-second centering is an excellent "mind approach" to healing and great to add to the other strategies you employ to keep yourself mentally and physically fit. You can use it to reduce stress, support healthy habits, and set yourself on a healing path. The Centering Sequence is especially helpful in promoting health. The following are the kinds of "work" you might name in the work-naming step of the sequence:

(I am feeling) (stronger)

(My wrist) (is healing)

(I envision) (good health)

(I am growing) (stronger)

(I am caring) (for my body)

(My back) (is getting better)

(My cold) (will pass)

(My health) (is returning)

What we say in the mind influences our physical and emotional health. Affirming how we'd like to feel and reducing negative self-talk reduce the risk of stress-related ailments and opportunistic infections. Not every physical ailment or emotional problem will respond to a mind/body approach, but a great many will and do. Starting today, enlist your mind in support of your physical and emotional health and do yourself a great favor.

A simple way to use ten-second centering and the Centering Sequence to promote physical and emotional health is to name "I am taking a walk" as the work you intend to do. Light and exercise are the best natural antidepressants we possess and taking even a twenty-minute walk is a terrific mood elevator. As an experiment, use the Centering Sequence to support your intention to take a walk. See if the act of centering helps motivate you to get out and stroll. Try this little mood elevation experiment today.

DAN

"I find myself in the summer staying inside when I'm not out performing. I'm sun sensitive and shy away from the sun, so it takes extra effort to expose myself to this necessary nutrient. I thought about the walking experiment but couldn't quite make myself try it. Actually, I felt exhausted and took a nap. When I awoke, though, I felt ready. It was late afternoon but it was also a beautiful day. I used the phrase 'ready for sun' when I named

my work. I set my stopwatch for twenty minutes and took a long route from my house to the park. I enjoyed the sun and the warm breeze but soon found negative thoughts intruding. I refocused on the beautiful day but found myself continually pulled back by the negatives. So I stopped completely and did the Centering Sequence right there in the park. When I got home, and in spite of the mixed emotions I'd experienced during the walk, I felt relaxed and energized. I made a short list of things to do that evening and I ended up doing four out of five."

CHARLENE

"I love the idea of using the Centering Sequence to spur me on to take a walk. I used the sequence before taking a twenty-minute walk this afternoon and it worked beautifully. I went walking alone and spent time thinking about solving some problems I was having with my writing. It felt wonderful to be walking, working, and enjoying myself all at the same time!"

Centering and Physical Health

You can use Ten Zen Seconds in a variety of ways to help yourself mentally and physically. Here are some reports from clients and study subjects on their healing tactics.

SHELLEY

"Currently I'm healing a strained leg that was hurt after playing a game of tennis. Not only am I using the incantations but I'm also getting Feldenkrais treatments, acupuncture, and physical therapy. With my current attention to centering and employing affirmative incantations, my confidence in being able to heal myself is high. I'm continuing to say, 'I feel absolutely wonderful,' as a nightly affirmation along with the incantations I've begun using. I know that it all works together."

Having the incantations available boosts confidence, which in turn boosts healing. The more you make Ten Zen Seconds a part of your life, the more confident you'll feel about effectively handling the ailments that come your way.

LARRY

"I've tried a 'mind' approach to physical healing many times. For instance, when I've felt the tickle of a cold or flu coming on I've been able to fend it off by repeating 'I will not get sick' and 'I

cannot get sick.' I realize that these are somewhat negative affir-mations, but they've worked often enough that I am hesitant about giving them up. I usually use them at times when I'm extremely busy with important deadlines approaching. Now I've taken to using the incantations in the same way. When I feel a cold coming on, I breathe-and-think 'I trust my resources' and 'I return with strength' and take some Vitamin C. This way I've been able to ward off colds this whole cold season."

The incantations work as preventive medicine. Centering not only helps you ward off stress-related illness but even reduces your chance of catching cold.

PAMELA

"After having healed a torn Achilles tendon, now I have to con-tend with a herniated disk at L-3 and bulging disks at L-4 and L-5. I have degenerative disk disease. Everything I can do to remain centered is a good thing. It's imperative for me to main-tain proper posture, to exercise, to stretch, and to keep moving. But I have a desk job, so it's very important for me to be in touch with my body. I'm using the Centering Sequence to remind me of what I need to do as I sit at my desk. I'm also using the incantation 'I am taking action' to get me up and stretching several times a day. Because of the chronic pain, I'm

also using 'I am open to joy' to help improve my mood and keep me from obsessing about what's ailing me."

Maybe you have to take medicine several times a day to control an illness. Maybe you engage in several stints of physical therapy a day to heal from an injury. You can turn these tasks into part of your centering practice by breathing-and-thinking your favorite incantation beforehand and by using Incantation 12, 'I return with strength,' to complete your healing ceremony.

FRANK

"This morning I was doing the Centering Sequence, using the phrase 'I am awaking with energy' as my work phrase, when the phone rang in the middle. I turned my head the wrong way to see who was calling and strained a muscle. Suddenly I had a physical ailment. Normally I would do some quick stretches and then get back to work. This time I did the sequence using the phrase 'My neck is relaxing.' That did a nice job of checking my habitual response to neck strains, a response that usually causes more problems for me down the road. I stayed seated and did some very slow, gentle exercises that helped to relax my neck muscles. I ended by doing another Centering Sequence using the phrase 'I am healing my neck.' The sequence slowed me down enough that I could take the time to be proactive, so in a very concrete way my

mind healed my body. I discovered that 'my neck is relaxing' was not only my desired state but the work that I had to do."

Centering helps you pay attention when an injury occurs or an illness strikes. By centering and calming yourself you give yourself the best chance possible of taking the right healing action.

Centering and Mental Health

Centering also helps with your mental health. You can use it as part of your process of recovering from an addiction, employing phrases like "I am clean and sober," "One day at a time," and "First things first" as the Centering Sequence work you name. You can use it to calm a mild mania or to lighten your mood when the blues strike. You can use it to counteract pessimism and negativity and, by affirming your intention to make meaning, ease existential difficulties. Its uses for emotional and mental health purposes are limitless. Here are a few reports.

HELEN

"When I'm feeling low and want to pull myself out of a debilitating mood, I often sit down and go over the Centering Sequence. Sometimes I also tack on other self-affirmations to restore my flagging energy. I'm pleased to report that doing the Centering Sequence

is a reliable way of dissipating my lethargy and lifting my spirits. Going through it may be the most effective way I have of getting quickly recharged because it helps me focus on what I want to do or need to do. That refocusing seems to be a sure-fire mood elevator."

Several of the incantations spur you to take action, which is often a complete mood elevator. When you feel lethargic, bored, or blue, get some meaningful work in mind, name it using Incantation 3, and then add Incantation 8, 10, or 11 ('I make my meaning,' 'I am equal to this challenge,' or 'I am taking action') to stir your blood and get you moving.

DONNA

"I started using the incantations at the peak of stress. I'd just had two months of intense stress due to a family member's hospitalization, financial crises, animal emergencies, and personal attacks from some coworkers at the office. I was under such stress that I could not function at all. In fact, I had just written to a friend to beg her for the secrets of living a balanced life. The universe had been sending me SOS messages to check out meditation and these messages were coming increasingly frequently as my health was failing. This is the frame of mind I was in when I started ten-second centering. It immediately addressed my concerns and my most dysfunctional states. I'd

already recognized everything you talk about but it was so much clearer in this particular 'package.' I was ready to make a change, I knew what direction I needed to go in, and ten-second centering matched that direction perfectly. It has become a key tool in helping me recover and maintain my physical and emotional health."

No doubt you've learned a lot from experience about what helps you maintain your emotional equilibrium and mental health. But insight usually isn't enough. You also need easy-to-understand, easy-to-use practices. Ten-second centering fits that bill.

TOM

"I'm mainly using ten-second centering to reduce anxiety. I'm trying to get in the habit of using the incantations every day to rid me of the anxiety that is always throwing me off center. In addition to the incantations I've been practicing the Centering Sequence and using the phrases 'relaxed and calm' and 'little acts of bravery' in the name-your-work step. Centering doesn't eliminate all the anxiety in my life but it gives me a sense of control and power and reduces my anxiety to much more manageable levels."

Anxiety is a major mental health issue and ten-second centering can be a key tool in helping you manage your anxious thoughts and feelings. The deep breathing component reduces anxiety. The thought component also reduces anxiety. Together they are an anxiety-management charm.

SARA

"It's surprised me how the whole experience of ten-second centering works so well for me. It sparks my energy, helps boost my mood, even gets me to go walking, and helps keep me clear on what I want to be doing. Because the practice has been valuable in boosting my energy and has proven to be effective in helping me maintain my drive and productivity, I find myself willing to use it more and more regularly. I consider it quite a healing gift. The power of the mind is phenomenal!"

Healing begins with the mind. The incantations are right thoughts that promote mental and physical health.

---

centering for performance

We all find ourselves performing in public, whether our performances are presentations at work, cocktail-hour conversations with acquaintances, phone calls on sales leads, or romantic dates. With performing comes performance anxiety. The territory of performance anxiety includes the anxiety we associate with musical, theatrical, and dance performances and also the anxiety we experience in business situations and interpersonal relationships. It's a territory that includes well-known performers and also tens of millions of ordinary people. Indeed, when people are surveyed about their phobias, invariably heading the list—before a fear of flying, a fear of snakes, or any other fear—is a fear of public speaking. The odds are good that performance anxiety is an issue for you.

The territory of performance anxiety also includes a great many people who regularly avoid performing. In order to avoid the experience of anxiety, they make it their business to avoid performance situations. So for them the issue of performance anxiety remains a hidden one. If you currently mask your performance anxiety by avoiding performance situations, you may have a problem with performance anxiety without even knowing it.

It's also possible that you're experiencing performance anxiety but not labeling it as such. A high school teacher I saw as a client would work until midnight preparing her lessons and always came to class overprepared. She nevertheless never felt prepared. It turned out that because she held teaching as a performance for which she needed a perfect script, she never felt free to improvise, relax, or "just let the kids discuss things." Once she realized that performance anxiety was her issue she began to make more modest preparations, interact more with her students, and enjoy teaching more.

I worked with a psychotherapist who sang on the side and who claimed to experience little anxiety when he performed. But among his presenting issues were periodic panic attacks and other anxiety symptoms. His symptoms made me wonder if performance anxiety might be a hidden issue in his life. As it happened, we attended a networking meeting at which participants had to introduce themselves. Mild anxiety is natural in such situations but my client could barely stammer out his introduction. It became clear that performance anxiety was indeed a significant issue in his life. Once he recognized this, admitted to the problem, and we began working on it, he was able to return to his stalled singing career.

What seems to frighten us about performing? Performance anxiety certainly has its reasons, but its reasons aren't as straightforward as, "plane might crash, therefore I would die," or, "Loose tiger, better run!" What bothers us about performing are the following sorts of things: that we might fail, that we might look foolish, that we might suffer a blow to our self-esteem, and so on. The list of possible fears about performing is very long. That's actually good to know. It's good to know that a lot may be going on inside of us, psychologically speaking, contributing to our experience of performance anxiety.

Performance anxiety occurs when a person consciously or unconsciously labels a given situation as a performance and, for whatever reasons, feels threatened by the situation. The experience of mild performance anxiety is well known to each of us. At such times we experience butterflies in the stomach, the need to urinate, a slight sense of disorientation, and similar physical symptoms. Before important or difficult performances we may react with more severe symptoms, moving from butterflies to nausea or from slight disorientation to a full "spacey" state.

Each anxious person, whether experiencing mild, moderate, or severe anxiety, has his or her own individual "package" of physical symptoms and distressing thoughts. The actress Maureen Stapleton explained, "When I'm in a play, the anxiety starts about six-thirty at night. I start to burp. I belch—almost nonstop. I keep burping, right up to the curtain, and then I'm all right. If a truck backfires, I jump. I can hear everything. I get scared that something is going to fall down or that there's going to be an explosion. I'm nervous every night, but opening night is even more of a nightmare. There's so much at stake that it just overpowers you."

Among the most common symptoms of performance anxiety are sweaty palms, a dry mouth, increased heart rate, shaky hands, weak knees, shortness of breath, butterflies in the stomach, and an increased need to use the bathroom. Psychological symptoms include feelings of confusion, disorientation, powerlessness, and loneliness. Some performers report briefly going deaf or blind. Additional psychological symptoms include the desire to escape or to hide, feelings of impending doom or death, or feelings of unreality. The singer Rosa Ponselle, for example, recalled, "I actually prayed that a car would run me over so that I wouldn't have to die onstage—a prayer that I was to repeat before every performance for twenty years."

The cellist Pablo Casals wrote in his autobiography *Joys and Sorrows*, "I gave my first real concert in Barcelona when I was fourteen. I was terribly nervous. When we got to the concert hall, I said, 'Father, I've forgotten the beginning of the piece! I can't remember a note of it! What shall I do?' He calmed me down. That was eighty years ago but I've never conquered that dreadful feeling of nervousness before a performance. It is always an ordeal. Before I go onstage, I have a pain in my chest. I'm tormented."

If you suffer from performance anxiety, my hunch is that you probably haven't come up with an effective tool to help you calm and center yourself before you perform. Most likely you've either white-knuckled performances, simply suffering with your anxiety and your painful symptoms, or you've resorted to alcohol or other drugs (including prescription ones) to try to quell your anxious feelings. There really is something better to try, namely Ten Zen Seconds.

Performance Anxiety and Centering

You can reduce your experience of performance anxiety by using the incantations to center yourself before you perform. Any one of the twelve can be used. After reading the following discussion, pick one or two incantations as your "stage fright charms" and then practice them, first in your mind's eye and then before you perform.

1. (I am completely) (stopping)

Because of anticipatory anxiety, you may keep yourself in a rush and avoid practicing your speech or your instrument. Use this incantation to calm yourself, stop yourself, and remind yourself that it is time to rehearse. Or you may find yourself "trapped" backstage before a performance and notice that your anxiety is mounting. Use this incantation as a way to "completely stop" your racing thoughts and calm yourself before you perform.

2. (I expect) (nothing)

By going into a performance not needing any particular outcome—not needing an error-free, perfect performance; a crescendo of applause when you finish; and so on—you reduce your experience of anxiety. Use this incantation to remind yourself that expectations are burdensome and a significant source of anxiety.

3. (I am) (doing my work)

Forthrightly naming the performance you're about to give and framing that work in a positive light are important calming strategies. You might choose (I will perform) (with strength), (I am ready) (to sing), (This audition) (will be excellent), or (I am excited) (to be acting).

4. (I trust) (my resources)

You may be adequately prepared to perform but not feel prepared. This incantation reminds you that you are indeed ready and in possession of everything you need in order to perform well. You can also use this incantation to assure yourself that fate and the alignment of the planets are on your side.

5. (I feel) (supported)

Rather than focusing on the negative aspects of a performance situation—for instance, that the room is smaller or colder than you would have liked—reorient yourself toward the positive, especially toward the humanness of your audience. You can also use this incantation as a shorthand reminder of your spiritual beliefs.

6. (I embrace) (this moment)

You can try to fight the moment and fervently wish that you were elsewhere. Or you can surrender, relax, and embrace the moment. Fighting the moment produces tension; embracing the moment produces lightness and calm. Use this incantation to fully accept that you are where you are.

7. (I am free) (of the past)

As you prepare for an upcoming performance, you may suddenly find yourself bombarded by unwelcome thoughts about past performances that went poorly, something in your childhood or upbringing that still haunts you, or some other memory or visceral sensation connected to the past. Use this incantation to rid yourself of that thought or feeling.

8. (I make) (my meaning)

Often when we experience anxiety about an upcoming performance we start to second-guess our reasons for performing, cast doubt on our motives, and precipitate a meaning crisis. This incantation helps remind us that our performances are necessary and even vital parts of our meaning-making efforts. Reassured that performing makes existential sense, you will discover your anxiety waning.

9. (I am open) (to joy)

This incantation helps remind you that there is joy to be found in the present moment and that you can experience making music, acting on stage, or presenting at work as a positive, joyous, heartfelt experience.

10. (I am equal) (to this challenge)

Many performers conceptualize their performance as a kind of heroic challenge that allows them to test their skills and their mettle. If you view performing this way, this incantation may work well for you. Even if you don't conceptualize performance as a battle, asserting that you are equal to the demands of the situation can prove a powerful calming thought.

11. (I am) (taking action)

Action reduces our experience of anxiety, which is one reason why performers tend to experience significantly less anxiety while performing than they do while waiting to perform. Virtually any action you take, whether it's walking around or stretching a few times, will reduce your experience of anxiety. This incantation reminds you that taking action is a powerful anxiety management tool.

12. (I return) (with strength)

Maybe your acting role calls for many exits and entrances or your part in the concert requires that you jump in dozens of times. This incantation helps you calm and center yourself as you await your next entrance or return. It also serves as an excellent "transition" incantation as you move from one performance situation to another throughout your day.

Many people find their careers hampered by their fear of performing and their personal lives diminished because they dread "performances" like dates, parties, and even conversing with their loved ones. Think through if performance anxiety is an issue for you. If it is, ten-second centering can help.

in the vanguard

It would flabbergast us to hear an indigenous person say that he didn't have time for his rain dance or his harvest festival. But if we learned that he'd just returned to his culture from a period abroad and was now cosmopolitan and college-educated, we'd understand. We'd understand that "not having time" really meant "I no longer find these rituals and ceremonies meaningful, even though I'm willing to pay them lip service." His change of mind and heart are the result of his exposure to a different culture, a different mind-set, and a different way of viewing the universe.

As an intellectual matter, I'm sure that you understand how Ten Zen Seconds might help you. If you haven't tried using the incantations yet, my hunch is that you've conceptualized the problem as a personal one, on the order of "I'm too lazy" or "I'm too undisciplined." But it's entirely likely that the lion's share of the blame rests with our culture's rules and the way we follow those unwritten rules. As a cultural matter, you have little or no permission to incorporate ten-second centering into your life.

This analysis may surprise you. But imagine the following. Say that your neighbor on the left started coming out every morning to spend a minute centering on the lawn. Then your neighbor on the right started doing the same each evening. Everyone in line at the supermarket unself-consciously centered, the clerks centered (even those checking the speed-through lines), your colleagues at work centered, virtually everyone you knew stopped for ten seconds here and there to gather themselves. Imagine this going on for long enough that no one remembered a time when people didn't stop to center. You would see what you see today in the relationship between Chinese culture and the practice of tai chi. Centering would become a cultural norm and an everyday practice.

Try the following mind experiment. Imagine that centering has become an integral part of our cultural fabric. Take a moment to visualize people centering as comfortably as, say, they pull out their cell phone. Imagine, further, that people not only stopped to center but actually became more centered. Imagine this as a beautiful culture-wide phenomenon. In this context, would you find Ten Zen Seconds an easier practice to follow? I'm sure that you would. Things that are culturally sanctioned are infinitely easier to do than things that aren't.

What isn't culturally sanctioned always requires a special effort—even a measure of heroism—to adopt. I'd like you to give ten-second centering a try in this cultural context. Your new role is as cultural pioneer. Not only will you be using the incantations to help yourself but you'll be breaking ground for others and initiating a new cultural norm. Wear this mantle of cultural pioneer. Help us all deepen our experience of life, quiet our nerves, and center.

Centering in the Vanguard

JEAN

"I have to say that I was feeling like a bit of a loser up to this point because I couldn't even follow through with this simple ten-second thing. I was just too embarrassed at this point to do anything with it. Hearing about cultural considerations freed me up quite a bit. I have since written out the Centering Sequence and stuck it onto my computer so that at least I now look at it. Thank you for the pardon. I now know that it's okay for me to start even if I've fallen behind and also that it's not some mystical experience but just a matter of calming myself down. Even though I'm at the starting gate, I no longer feel like a failure at something that takes only a few seconds!"

Don't underestimate the power of cultural injunctions. They stop us in our tracks. To center you will need to step outside the culture. Take that giant step.

RACHEL

"Suffering from a variety of physical and mental maladies due primarily to stress, I'd been searching for a way to slowly begin releasing stress and allow a gentler, me-centered pace to come into my life. So I thought I'd try ten-second centering. At least, that was the theory. Instead, I've been simply glancing through the lessons and hoping that I'd 'get to it eventually.' I even tried to take a day off to work on it, and although I found the incantations helpful I couldn't incorporate them into my daily life. Your discussion today, though, sparked a deeper interest for me. I am constantly examining the social reasons behind why people behave the way they do and I think you've hit on it exactly. Although it's exciting to be on the 'leading edge' of a trend, sometimes it can also be such a huge risk that it is easier to be resistant. But you're suggesting creating a community of support where centering is the norm, supported by Other, instead of outside of Other. I think this is why meditation and yoga groups do so well. We see others struggling, attempting, doing the practice, and so we feel validated to at least attempt the practice. The problem, of course, is that meetings are a rarified environment and often it can be difficult to practice outside the

meeting. What does this mean for me? Well, I wish that centering were culturally supported. The change must begin with me and ten-second centering is only one part of an entire holistic approach I'm attempting to create in my life."

Ten-second centering is an individual practice. Group centering would certainly support individual centering, just as AA groups support individual sobriety and yoga classes support individual practice. But ultimately you must take what you learn from a group and what you practice in a group and carry it out into the world. Join or start a ten-second centering group, if you like, but set your mind on individual practice.

THERESA

"I think you hit the nail on the head. I've often caught myself thinking that if I were surrounded by people who were centering or meditating, I wouldn't have half the problems I currently do trying to keep it in my life. I've heard about the effects of group consciousness, but I find it disturbing sometimes that I'm not strong enough to withstand the effects of cultural norms. It's going to take a while to undo forty years of brainwashing. I've felt so different and alien for so long that it's going to take some time to supplant 'oddball' and 'weirdo' with 'pioneer.' However, it's a cause that is well worth undertaking. I don't think I'll ever stop

feeling like an alien in this culture, but if I can manage to feel like an inspiration for other souls like me, that would be great."

You may be something of a cultural outsider. Outsiders can complain or lead. Lead by example. Bravely and conspicuously center in public. If someone asks you what you're doing, reply, "It's my centering practice." If they want to know more, teach them.

JANICE

"There was a time when I thought that I was prohibited from doing many things because of cultural customs. Then I believed that I was over those restrictions. Now I'm not so sure. The idea of not only helping myself become centered but helping others and our culture to become more grounded is a challenging and intriguing concept. If ten-second centering can help me become more present and more effective in what I do—and it can do the same for others—wouldn't that be wonderful? The idea of introducing ten-second centering to create more sanity in the world is most ambitious, a very large objective indeed. It is inspiring to imagine the possibility."

Hold the ambition to inspire others. But start with yourself. It is a long journey to get free of the culture in which we are embedded as every commercial and every news headline support cultural norms. To begin this journey, take the single step of owning one or two incantations and using them throughout the day.

FRANK

"I'm a conservative guy by nature and I have very few reservations about how this culture operates. I believe in our principles and our freedoms, though maybe we're just a little too free, and I like it that we are still a religious nation. I think that we have more to conserve than to change and that there are really two cultures, the one I see around me every day, which is conservative, and the one portrayed on television and in the movies, which is ten times more liberal than the people I know. But I'm not against ten-second centering. I don't see it as undermining traditional values or radical in any sense. I don't call your phrases 'incantations'—magic is not only not a part of my religion, it is expressly forbidden—but that's the only problem I have with the program. So it isn't necessary to be a cultural pioneer to get something from ten-second centering. You can be just normal and mainstream."

It isn't necessary to consider yourself a cultural pioneer in order to embrace Ten Zen Seconds, though embracing it may make you one! It only requires desire and practice.

MARSHA

"Last November I quit my government supervisor job of seventeen years to make a major change in my life—to become a full-time writer. People honestly thought I was crazy and didn't bother to be polite about it. They warned me that I'd go broke, that I'd be lonely working from home, that I'd be back because I would miss the money. I went from making $33 an hour to making $33 a day. I haven't missed that hellhole once in seven months, and, at this point, I am 100 percent certain that I'll never go back and will never miss the stress and machinations. In this culture, it's a badge of honor to work twelve hours a day, rush everywhere, be efficient while attending to loads of minutiae. And then people wonder why they have hypertension, heart attacks, panic attacks, and depression. Why they can't connect with their spouses, children, and extended family. Why they feel alone and like God has abandoned them. I've been there and I am not going back, even if I am considered odd. I have a hunch I'll live longer—or at least be happier while I am here on Earth. I no longer care if people think I am odd. I would rather be centered and content. I think what you said about things that are so obviously good for us being forbidden in our contemporary Western culture is totally true. And of course its culture-wide absence is connected to our fears about whether life is meaningful or a mere cosmic happenstance. Absolutely! Too few people take time to consider weighty issues, to connect meaningfully with other people, to consider the fact that we

are all ephemeral beings. How do we make the time we are here and the relationships with the people we love meaningful and rich? It surely isn't by sitting in traffic honking, shaking fists, and cursing at others who are in the same situation."

Help those around you by becoming more centered yourself. It's not easy being a cultural pioneer, but it may prove the most rewarding experience of your life.

Chapter Twenty-Eight

Your centering practice

The ten-second centering process is designed to do a number of important things, all in the space of a few seconds. Naturally you'll have to judge for yourself how well it works and how it compares and contrasts to centering strategies you may have employed in the past. If you've tried other centering strategies before, take a few minutes to think through how Ten Zen Seconds stacks up against those techniques. For instance, think through if you'd like to add a physical component, like ritual movement of the sort employed in yoga and tai chi, to your personal centering routine. Would you like to add a brief relaxation component, as brief as rubbing your neck or momentarily visualizing a calming scene? Throughout this book I've asked you to take responsibility for customizing ten-second centering, and another excellent place to take responsibility is in the area of adding additional features that will make the process work better for you.

ELAINE

"In the past I've used a centering method that included listening to a ten-minute audiotape that helped you relax your whole body, from your toes to the top of your head, and included visual imagery to put your mind in a beautiful place. Another practice included repeating affirmations of my own choosing five times each. The primary strength for me of ten-second centering is its brevity, as well as the excellent sense that each incantation makes. In fact, once I started using the incantations, I immediately began to focus on the things that I wanted to get done. I didn't have to go through a whole set of relaxation practices before getting on with it. I think that all of the methods I've used previously have been effective in their own way, but the simplicity and the depth of ten-second centering distinguishes it from other practices. So I'm not feeling the need to add anything to the process, as it's working beautifully as is."

VERONICA

"In the past the centering technique I used the most was taking a visualization vacation break where I imagined myself in a relaxing, exotic location. I would close my eyes and feel the sun shine down on me. At the same time I would visualize roots sprouting from the soles of my feet and going deeply into the earth. This technique didn't include breath awareness and there were no particular

thoughts associated with the exercise, although after 'transporting' myself into this vacation locale I would sometimes concentrate on an affirmation. The 'rooting' tends to give me an overall grounding experience and sometimes it's just nice to have a pretend escape and adventure. But ten-second centering has its own virtues. What I especially like about it is that it can be done anywhere. Your eyes don't have to be closed, it isn't obvious that you're using it, and it isn't time-consuming. It does the job nicely and offers a wide range of customization. But I think I may add the visualization component, as I miss those mini-vacations!"

RHONDA

"Yesterday I came to the office to find a work colleague in a real snit of anxiety. Instead of lecturing her I just calmed her down with a quick hit of Reiki to the back of the neck for five minutes while chanting the mantra 'I am completely stopping' in my own mind. It was as if my thoughts could mind-meld with hers and she somehow could absorb Incantation 1 that way, without me actually having to say it out loud. I went through all the incantations in my own mind as I Reikied her. After she was totally relaxed and ready to move back into her work, I told her that whenever she felt this overwhelming anxiety she could just think 'I am completely stopping' and breathe in. I didn't even mention breathing out, because that is an automatic physical response that eventually has to happen. At

the end of the day she said that she'd felt great all day and that when she felt her frustration rising she would think of my Reiki hands at the back of her neck and the words 'I am completely stopping.' As a Reiki Master, centering is an important part of beginning a session with a student. But it has to be taught and learned because the average person doesn't give herself permission to 'stop' even for a moment. This is where I think ten-second centering can be so effective. It's quick. It's easy. It works. It's as simple as breathing. I intend to incorporate it into my Reiki teaching and much more."

MARTHA

"I've tried Insight Meditation and it seems to have the advantage of not promoting thinking. Thinking is my thing and I have the existential problems and frustrations to prove it. I've also tried repeating mantras, repeating words, chanting, yoga, journaling, walking, breath work, and many other things. All of them worked somewhat and my best success with a few of them seemed to come while driving. But I didn't use any of them consistently enough to establish the habit or the practice. The incantations have strengths that these other practices didn't have. I love their immediacy and that there's no need to set aside a lot of time or the private space required with meditation. You can use them frequently throughout the day because it takes less mental and physical preparation and can be integrated into your day without advanced planning. I also find the

thoughts very calming and they give my monkey mind something to focus on, which really does help me be much less distracted."

Although you may want to acquire additional centering strategies, Ten Zen Seconds can serve as your complete centering regimen. Personalize it so that it fits the bill and then practice using it until it becomes habitual. Your goal is to know to stop completely when stopping completely is what will help center you, to trust your resources when trusting your resources is what's needed, and so on. Over the course of a single long, deep breath you can still your nerves, marshal your wits, and prepare for any challenge.

Not Worrying about Failing

If ten-second centering makes sense to you, why wouldn't you give it a try? Possibly because you fear failing. How many times have you broken resolutions, slipped off diets, or failed to get up that hour earlier to exercise? We all have the same checkered past and the same memories of missteps.

Forgive yourself right now if you haven't added Ten Zen Seconds to your life and be open to the possibility that you will still give it a shot. Release old guilt and pain and get yourself on a positive, optimistic footing.

MARTHA

"Having abandoned things in the past makes it much harder to stick with new things. I feel that I'm already starting out with a handicap. Even as I decide I want to try something new, I'm already nearly convinced, 'Why bother? You know you'll never stick to it.' Then I know, too, that if I start it and don't finish, I'm going to feel even worse. So that's a lot of incentive to not even go there. It's very difficult to forgive myself for these past behaviors. I think that I see even appropriate forgiveness as a kind of white-washing or making excuses. I seem to think that to forgive myself in any way is to say that it's all right to be flighty and to not do what I say I'm going to do. It's all wrapped up in 'my word' and 'telling the truth' and even 'integrity.' I really beat myself up a lot over past failures and had no idea to what extent I was doing that. As you suggest, I'm going to approach ten-second centering in a different, more relaxed, and more optimistic way."

KATHY

"I'm giving myself great credit for doing the incantations daily. I acknowledge that as a great accomplishment as I've certainly abandoned many, many projects and plans. The memory of those 'failures' really does limit a person's hope at being able to succeed. I can think of too many attempts at healthy eating, regular exercise, etc. Some things that I abandoned—like the violin at age eleven—

haven't had much of an impact on me, but other things that I've abandoned, especially certain people, have made a profound impact. I tend to approach new things with a fear (almost an expectation) that I'll repeat the past. And when I do repeat the past and fail at something I feel very disappointed with myself. For me, it's almost impossible to forgive myself for abandoning those things. So I'm very pleased to have stuck with ten-second centering. It probably helps that it's simple and only takes ten seconds. Maybe it's built to be foolproof!"

Your Centering Journey

I hope that you've enjoyed learning about Ten Zen Seconds. I know that my coaching clients and study subjects benefit from learning about it and putting it into practice. Some have experienced small problems with the process—that it's taken some time to settle on the incantations that work best or remained a struggle to turn the process into a habit. But these small problems have not stopped them from practicing ten-second centering and, eventually, coming to rely on it.

It's never too late to begin a centering practice. Try Ten Zen Seconds today. At a minimum, pick one incantation that resonates for you and make it your own. This simple but powerful centering technique will make a profound, positive difference in your life.

About the Author

Eric Maisel, PhD, is the author of more than thirty works of fiction and nonfiction. His nonfiction titles include *Creativity for Life, Everyday You, Coaching the Artist Within, Fearless Creating, The Van Gogh Blues, The Creativity Book, Performance Anxiety, A Writer's Paris, A Writer's San Francisco,* and *Toxic Criticism.* A columnist for *Art Calendar* magazine and a regular contributor to *Art of the Song Creativity Radio,* Maisel is a San Francisco-based creativity coach and creativity coach trainer who presents keynote addresses and workshops nationally and internationally.

Maisel holds undergraduate degrees in philosophy and psychology, Master's degrees in counseling and creative writing, and a doctorate in counseling psychology. He is a California licensed marriage and family therapist, and founded and wrote *Callboard* magazine's "Staying Sane in the Theater" column. Maisel has presented at venues as diverse as the American Psychological Association annual conference, the Romance Writers of America annual conference, the San Francisco Conservatory of Music, the American Conservatory Theater, the North Carolina School of the Arts, and the Paris Writers Workshop.

Visit www.ericmaisel.com to learn more about Dr. Maisel, or write to the author at ericmaisel@hotmail.com. And please visit www.tenzenseconds.com, where you can learn more about Ten Zen methods. You might also like to subscribe to Dr. Maisel's free monthly Ten Zen Seconds newsletter; to subscribe, just drop an email to tenzenseconds-subscribe@yahoogroups.com.